Praise for *Questions are the Answer*

"Posner and Weems deliver an invaluable resource for anyone looking to navigate the complexities of the modern workplace. This book addresses critical leadership topics to make a meaningful difference in our organizations and the people we lead.

What sets this guidebook apart is its practical approach. Each chapter is not only filled with insightful strategies but also includes dedicated sections for self-evaluation, reflection, and how to move forward. This encourages continuous growth, helping readers to not just absorb the information but to actively engage with it and apply it in their own contexts.

Posner and Weems empower us to ask the right questions, which is essential in today's fast-paced environment. Their expertise shines through, making this book a must-read for leaders and professionals at all levels who are committed to leadership development. I wholeheartedly endorse this guidebook as a powerful tool for anyone seeking to enhance their leadership skills and drive positive change in their workplace."

—**Rhonda Caldwell, Ed.D.**
Executive Director, Kentucky Association of School Administrators

"After 25 years in sales and business development, I've learned that asking thoughtful questions is the most powerful way to earn trust, uncover real needs, and create lasting solutions for my prospects and clients. These ideas reframe the same ideas for leadership and self-improvement. They show how inquiry drives clarity and connection. The reminder that "we talk too much and don't ask enough" hit home. Asking the right questions of your organization and even of yourself isn't a weakness; it's the foundation of innovation and empathy."

—**Matt Watson**
Broker Impact & Engagement Advisor, Premiums for the Planet

"From practical examples to thought-provoking prompts, *Questions are the Answer* provides tools for growth no matter your job title, role, or responsibilities, and shows how to leverage the power of questions in any team—whether that's a marriage, a family, a small business, or a Fortune 500 company. It is a practical, thought-provoking guide that equips readers to grow, lead, and collaborate more effectively. This book is a powerful tool for anyone looking to elevate their impact—so much so that it will be required reading for all new hires in my organization."

—**Laura Kreuger**
Executive Director, Asset Locale

"This book captures something every leader learns sooner or later: progress doesn't begin with answers, it begins with questions. Reading this book reminded me how often leaders and teams move too quickly to solutions, when the real opportunity is in asking sharper, more intentional questions.

That truth has only become more relevant in today's environment, especially with the rise of AI. As we've learned that even the most advanced technology depends entirely on the quality of the questions (prompts) we ask. In other words, AI hasn't changed the importance of questions; it has magnified it. The better the question, the better the thinking, and the better the outcome.

The book's focus on leadership growth, decision-making, and managing change resonates deeply with my experience. For example, at my company, we use a decision-making framework known as the DAI model. What I've seen is that the real discipline isn't in deciding who has the "D," but in first clarifying what problem we're solving and what risks are at stake. That kind of framing happens only when we pause long enough to ask the right questions.

An excellent guide for leaders, managers, and innovators who want to strengthen that discipline—because the right questions don't just open the door to better answers; they are one of the most powerful management tools we have."

—**Jack Orville**
General Manager, Exact Sciences

"This book brilliantly shows that asking questions is not a weakness but a powerful tool for influence and understanding. With expert-curated, outcome-focused questions, this book equips leaders and teams alike to drive meaningful change—whether in the boardroom or everyday work."

—**Mercedes de Luca**
Chief Information Officer, Pebble Beach Resorts

"Posner and Weems astutely argue that the art of posing the right questions is fundamental to overcoming challenges, fostering innovation, and guiding sound decision-making across all organizational settings. This is a must-read for anyone serious about organizational excellence."

—**Earl W. Stafford**
Founder and CEO, The Wentworth Group, LLC

"Posner and Weems approach to leadership is both insightful and refreshingly authentic, and they seamlessly blend practical wisdom with the art of asking meaningful questions. This book stands out as a beacon for anyone striving to enhance not only their own leadership skills but also to inspire growth and innovation within their teams and organizations.

By emphasizing the power of questions, the book invites readers to rethink traditional leadership paradigms. Instead of focusing solely on answers or directives, the authors encourage leaders to cultivate curiosity, active listening, and thoughtful dialogue. This, in turn, promotes a culture of continuous learning and constructive collaboration.

What truly distinguishes this book are the practical tools and reflective exercises interwoven throughout each chapter. The book masterfully guides readers through scenarios that illuminate the complexities of leadership in today's fast-paced and ever-evolving environments. The blend of research, real-world examples, and actionable strategies makes the book accessible and highly relevant for leaders at all stages of their journey.

In conclusion, this book is a must-read for anyone interested in elevating their leadership practice. It is both a guide and an inspiration, reminding us that great leaders are not defined by the answers they possess but by the questions they are willing to ask. I wholeheartedly recommend this book and commend Posner and Weems for this outstanding contribution to the field of leadership."

—Anne Moser
Principal, Mosser Summit Strategies

"Leadership does not fail for a lack of answers. It fails when leaders stop asking the right questions. Posner and Weems powerfully illustrate how curiosity becomes the engine of strategy, culture, and real growth."

—Scott K. Edinger
Wall Street Journal and *USA Today* bestselling author of
The Growth Leader

"These days, change is happening at all levels and at all times. This is an excellent read to help ensure we're asking the right questions to get the answers we need, and getting those answers will help effectively lead our organizations through successful change. And because one can lead, regardless of one's level, this is a book that can help anyone."

—Caroline Chang
Vice President, Advancement, Kindsight

Questions
are the
Answer

BARRY Z. POSNER • LOVETT H. WEEMS

Questions *are the* Answer

Learning How To **ASK** Rather Than **TELL**

WILEY

Copyright © 2026 by Barry Z. Posner and Lovett H. Weems. All rights reserved.

Published by John Wiley & Sons, Inc., Hoboken, New Jersey.

No part of this publication may be reproduced, stored in a retrieval system, or transmitted in any form or by any means, electronic, mechanical, photocopying, recording, scanning, or otherwise, except as permitted under Section 107 or 108 of the 1976 United States Copyright Act, without either the prior written permission of the Publisher, or authorization through payment of the appropriate per-copy fee to the Copyright Clearance Center, Inc., 222 Rosewood Drive, Danvers, MA 01923, (978) 750-8400, fax (978) 750-4470, or on the web at www.copyright.com. Requests to the Publisher for permission should be addressed to the Permissions Department, John Wiley & Sons, Inc., 111 River Street, Hoboken, NJ 07030, (201) 748-6011, fax (201) 748-6008, or online at http://www.wiley.com/go/permission.

The manufacturer's authorized representative according to the EU General Product Safety Regulation is Wiley-VCH GmbH, Boschstr. 12, 69469 Weinheim, Germany, e-mail: Product_Safety@wiley.com.

Trademarks: Wiley and the Wiley logo are trademarks or registered trademarks of John Wiley & Sons, Inc. and/or its affiliates in the United States and other countries and may not be used without written permission. All other trademarks are the property of their respective owners. John Wiley & Sons, Inc. is not associated with any product or vendor mentioned in this book.

Limit of Liability/Disclaimer of Warranty: While the publisher and the authors have used their best efforts in preparing this work, including a review of the content of the work, neither the publisher nor the authors make any representations or warranties with respect to the accuracy or completeness of the contents of this work and specifically disclaim all warranties, including without limitation any implied warranties of merchantability or fitness for a particular purpose. No warranty may be created or extended by sales representatives, written sales materials or promotional statements for this work. The fact that an organization, website, or product is referred to in this work as a citation and/or potential source of further information does not mean that the publisher and authors endorse the information or services the organization, website, or product may provide or recommendations it may make. This work is sold with the understanding that the publisher is not engaged in rendering professional services. The advice and strategies contained herein may not be suitable for your situation. You should consult with a specialist where appropriate. Further, readers should be aware that websites listed in this work may have changed or disappeared between when this work was written and when it is read. Neither the publisher nor authors shall be liable for any loss of profit or any other commercial damages, including but not limited to special, incidental, consequential, or other damages.

For general information on our other products and services or for technical support, please contact our Customer Care Department within the United States at (800) 762-2974, outside the United States at (317) 572-3993 or fax (317) 572-4002.

Wiley also publishes its books in a variety of electronic formats. Some content that appears in print may not be available in electronic formats. For more information about Wiley products, visit our web site at www.wiley.com.

Library of Congress Cataloging-in-Publication Data is Available:

ISBN 9781394429943 (Cloth)
ISBN 9781394429950 (ePub)
ISBN 9781394429967 (ePDF)

Cover Design: Jon Boylan
Cover Image: © creo2/stock.adobe.com
Author Photos: Courtesy of the Authors
Printed and bound by CPI Group (UK) Ltd, Croydon, CR0 4YY
C9781394429943_160326

Contents

Preface		*xiii*
Chapter 1	**Why Questions are the Answer**	1
Chapter 2	**Growing as a Leader**	9
	Seeking Feedback	11
	Legacy	13
	Self-Evaluation	14
	Reflection	16
	Continuing to Grow	17
Chapter 3	**Facing Challenges**	21
	Getting Started	23
	Thinking Outside the Box	25
	Identifying Resources	27
	Connecting to Purpose	29
	Monitoring Progress	31
	Evaluating Performance	31
	Fostering Learning	33
	Creative Abandonment	34
	Testing Routines	36

Contents

Chapter 4	**Leading Change**	**39**
	Understanding Your Organization's Identity	41
	Planning for Change	43
	Opportunities and Challenges	44
	What If?	46
	Focusing	50
	Learning Agenda	52
Chapter 5	**Innovation**	**57**
	Leading Innovation	58
	Encouraging Creativity	61
	Assessing the Past and Present	63
	Anticipating the Future	66
Chapter 6	**Making Good Decisions**	**71**
	Getting Started	73
	Testing Assumptions	74
	Exploring Options	76
	Assessing the Impact	79
Chapter 7	**Personnel Matters**	**83**
	When There's an Opening	84
	Interviewing	86
	Assessing Candidates	89
	Removing Barriers	91
	Engaging	94
	Handling Differences	97
Chapter 8	**Management Still Matters**	**103**
	The Best Managers Are Also Leaders	105
	Leaders Must Have Some Degree of Management Competency	107
	Planning	108
	Making the Most of Meetings	111
	Delegation	113
	Time Management	117

Chapter 9	**Communication**	**121**
	Self-Reflection	122
	Making Connections	125
	Listening	128
Chapter 10	**Making a Difference**	**137**
	Purpose	138
	Intentionality	140
	The Leader's Role	143

Suggested Reading — *149*
About the Authors — *153*

Preface

It seems appropriate to begin this book with a question that you are probably asking yourself:

Why should I read this book?

It is a reasonable question.

To which we would respond, not with an answer but with another set of questions, such as:

Why do you buy and read books to begin with?

What do you want to learn?

What would make you even more effective?

Another question you might ask us is, "Why did you write this book?"

To this, we would respond, "because knowing how to ask the right questions opens up a world of possibilities."

Think about the word *question* itself. The word, according to the dictionary, is a noun (and it can also be a verb) defined as "a sentence in an interrogative form, addressed to someone in order to get information in reply." Synonyms include *inquiry, quiz, probe, examine, investigate, interrogate,* and *query*; while antonyms include *respond, reply, answer*, and *explain*. As a leader, your questions send the receiver on a "quest"—directing them in a particular path, highlighting a focus, or emphasizing an issue that necessitates a response.

Don't you often ask yourself before responding to someone's question, "What's the point of that question I'm being asked?" or even "What's the *real* question *behind* that question?" When you ask someone a question, what is your point?

The questions you ask not only can change your life but also the lives of others. From a leadership perspective, the questions you ask people set a pattern for their thinking and a roadmap signaling to them what's important to you. Indeed, leaders, especially, need to be intentional about the *first* question they ask, because it sets the stage for what follows in the conversation. Consider the difference in focus and emphasis when you start your staff meeting by asking, "How much did we sell last quarter?" versus "How will changing customer habits affect our business in five years?" Or, ask, "What are we learning from our customer experience surveys?" versus "What's the latest innovation coming from R&D these days?"

We have organized the book around some of the most essential and critical issues facing people in any organizational context or environment—whether public or private, large or small—and, regardless of your personality, age, gender, ethnicity, function, or position (e.g., management or individual contributor). These factors may be worthy of consideration in how you execute the question (e.g., tone), but for the most part, the question remains the question.

Chapter 1 explains why the questions you ask matter. How considering the questions you want to ask on a particular topic or issue can help you achieve the "quest" (the end goal) you had in mind and make the difference you want. Chapter 2 focuses on questions to ask yourself as you develop your leadership skills, abilities, and mindset. Chapter 3 considers how to best address the inevitable challenges you will face, from problem and opportunity identification through to learning from experience and, sometimes, letting go. Chapter 4 moves beyond challenge to understanding how to lead change efforts.

As a necessary part of living in today's volatile, uncertain, complex, and ambiguous (VUCA) world, you must focus attention on

Preface

being innovative, which is the aim of Chapter 5. Making good decisions is an integral part of everyone's job, and the process, from getting started to assessing impact, is identified in Chapter 6. Managers and leaders face a great many personal and "personnel" issues, and this is true even for individual contributors. Chapter 7 offers clues about how to deal with many of them.

While we focus on exercising leadership throughout the book, Chapter 8 is a reminder that effective management still makes a difference, regardless of function or hierarchical level. What may have seemed implicit throughout these chapters—communications—is the focus of Chapter 9. It involves a great deal more than simply telling people what to do. The book concludes in Chapter 10 by asking you to consider, broadly speaking, what it is you care enough about that it would warrant your time, talents, and energies.

In some ways, the book can be a quick read; you can start in any chapter and skip around any topics within the chapter. There is nothing that needs to be memorized. It would be beneficial to have an issue (organizational or personal) in mind as you read, allowing you to identify questions and perspectives that will enhance your effectiveness in approaching problems and people. There is nothing magical or tricky about the questions; every one of them has stood the test of time and experience. We hope you will discover a few that you hadn't previously considered—and that we have now persuasively answered your question of why you should read this book.

—Barry Z. Posner
Berkeley, California

—Lovett H. Weems
Washington, DC.

1 Why Questions are the Answer

The leader of the past was a person who knew how to tell.
The leader of the future will be a person who knows how to ask.
—Peter Drucker[1]

Millions saw the apple fall, but Newton was the one who asked why.
—Barnard Baruch[2]

In a sleek office tower nestled in the heart of a bustling city, two employees worked side by side in the Strategy Department of a large corporation.

One was Mara, a rising analyst known for her relentless curiosity. She asked questions—lots of them. Some found her inquiries tedious, but her manager appreciated her hunger to understand.

The other was Jeff, a charismatic senior associate. Jeff was the kind of person people listened to. He had answers ready before a question was even fully formed. Clients trusted him, and junior staff admired his confident presentations.

One day, the team encountered a significant problem. A long-standing client had abruptly withdrawn from a partnership, citing dissatisfaction. The CEO demanded answers about why this happened and what was going to be done about it by the end of the week.

Jeff took the lead. "They didn't see the value," he declared confidently in the team meeting. "Our model must've confused them. Let's simplify it and repackage."

Mara raised a hand. "Do we know why they left? Has anyone actually asked them?"

Jeff shrugged. "We can guess. We know the product. Let's focus on fixing what we think went wrong."

But Mara wasn't satisfied. She spent a day calling the client's team. She asked open-ended questions—about their expectations, their experience, their goals. She listened.

What she found surprised everyone.

"It wasn't the model," Mara reported. "It was the assumptions we made about their needs. We talked too much. We didn't ask enough. They felt unheard."

The room fell silent.

Jeff cleared his throat. "But I've been talking to them for months."

Mara nodded. "Talking to them. Not with them."

That week, the team restructured their strategy, not based on assumptions but on real insights born from better questions. The client returned, this time feeling valued.

Later that evening, as they packed up for the day, Jeff turned to Mara. "I forgot how much we used to ask questions as kids," he said. "Somewhere along the way, I started thinking having the answers mattered more."

Mara smiled. "The right answer can only come from the right question. Knowing how to ask—that's where it starts."

And from then on, the team didn't just chase solutions. They chased understanding.

Moral: Before you can find the correct answer, you must first learn to ask the right question.

This paradox occurs throughout organizations, even at the most senior levels, as exemplified by the reflections of Martin Luther King Jr. In discussing the need for a voting rights bill with Presidents John F. Kennedy and his successor, Lyndon B. Johnson, he recalled that the former asked questions for an hour, while the latter spoke for an hour: "That's the difference between them."[3] Just like Mara and Jeff.

Asking questions, so easily practiced when we are children, who often drive parents, teachers, and adults generally batty with questions of "why?" (estimated at asking around 30 questions per hour), gives way to reticence as we grow older. We begin to assume that asking questions is a sign of weakness, that it makes us feel vulnerable, and that only people who don't know what is going on are the ones who ask questions. We look around and presume we're in some sort of competition with our co-workers, and if they aren't asking any questions, we don't want to ask ourselves for fear of appearing stupid or unprepared. "Smart" people, you say to yourself, don't have to ask questions because they already know the answers. Think about what people do these days when they stumble across something they don't know. Most would rather ask Siri, Alexa, or Google or spend 15 minutes with ChatGPT figuring it out, than five minutes asking around the office and admitting it's not in their skill set yet.

Researchers have found that asking questions, particularly seeking advice, actually makes people appear more competent and intelligent to others.[4] This somewhat counterintuitive finding stems from the positive impact on the person being asked for advice, who often feels flattered and assumes the questioner is insightful for seeking their expertise. Few things bring more satisfaction to someone than to be asked something about which they have knowledge or experience; it feels good: "They're asking what I think because they believe I'm smart and I know the answer. In turn, I think they're smart for asking because I'm going to tell them things that will be useful." Additionally, individuals who ask questions are often perceived as more likable and engaged, which leads to more positive interpersonal interactions.

There's this myth that as we grow up, as we move up the organizational ladder, we are supposed to know the answers to "everything." We assume, moreover, that no one wants to answer our questions or that we don't want to embarrass anyone by asking something for which they might not readily have an answer. Given their own fears of not knowing what to say, others are as reluctant to solicit questions as we are to ask them freely.

When you ask questions, you send the recipient on a mental journey. Your questions choose the path that people will follow and focus their search for answers. If you were to ask, for example, "How are you partnering with a colleague on getting this project completed?" you are sending a signal about the importance of collaboration. If you ask, "What have you done today to reduce the costs of doing business?" you are sending a very different message. Both are legitimate questions, but they indicate very different priorities. Your questions let people know what is top of mind for you and how they should be directing their attention and energy.

In *Leadership Conversations: Challenging High-Potential Managers to Become Great Leaders*, the authors point out that in a neurological sense, your mom was correct when she complained, "Everything I tell you goes in one ear and out the other. If she had asked questions instead, you would have retained more of her messages. That is because the brain functions with the obstinacy of a child: tell it what to do, and it starts analyzing the implications; if, instantly, you ask the brain a question, it will treat it as a problem to be solved—a game to be played. People like solving problems because doing so gives them a rush when the brain releases neurotransmitters that act like adrenaline."[5]

The lesson for leaders, they maintain, is to "ask your people questions and let them decide the course of action, rather than telling them what to do, how to do it, and when it should be done." Asking questions is a vital part of the repertoire of the most effective leaders, whose conversations are littered with questions.

Many scholars have echoed this observation and point out that "questioning is a uniquely powerful tool" that promotes the exchange of ideas, fosters learning, drives innovation, and builds rapport and trust.[6] A leader's questions highlight particular issues and concerns, and they send messages. They ask people to consider specific focus areas, such as operating costs, customer service, inclusion, quality, trust, or market share. Questions provide information about which values to attend to and how much energy should be devoted to them. They point people in a specific direction. The first question you ask is an obvious indicator of direction and priority. When the area manager for a large public utility firm wanted her team to shift their focus from revenue to customer satisfaction, she ensured that every staff meeting began with questions centered on how customers were feeling about their services and products.

Asking questions in the context of design thinking is referred to as *problem finding*. It is the crucial first step in understanding the user's needs and identifying the core issues before attempting to find solutions. It's about actively seeking out the real problems that need to be addressed, rather than jumping to conclusions or relying on assumptions. This involves empathizing with users, observing their behaviors, and gathering insights to define a clear and actionable problem statement.[7]

Your use of questions also develops people. Questions help them escape the trap of their mental models by broadening their perspectives in thinking about and taking responsibility for their responses. Additionally, you are required to listen attentively to what people are saying when asking them questions or otherwise you are demonstrating disrespect for their ideas and opinions.

If you are genuinely interested in what others think, you should ask for their opinions. Asking others for their thoughts facilitates participation in the decision-making process and consequently increases support for that decision ("answer"). The manager of a sporting goods store recognized the need to engage every employee in developing ideas to improve sales. For example, he asked each of them to go to the product wall and select the skis or snowboard they wanted. After giving them a few minutes to make their decisions, he asked them to close their eyes and envision what it would look like to use the new gear: "Feel the cold. Hear the wind whistle. Smell the fresh mountain air." His questions prompted them to consider how most people make emotional (rather than technical) purchase decisions.

He used questions to reframe the staff's thinking and their approach to sales. As the noted scholar and consultant Ed Schein observed, "My teaching and consulting experience has taught me that what builds a relationship, what solves problems, what moves things forward is asking the right questions."[8]

What most people in general, and leaders in particular, need is more practice in developing and asking the kinds of questions that draw usefully from the wisdom of their colleagues and constituents, enabling their thinking and resolve to move forward. To be effective, leaders must first establish a strong bond with their co-workers and constituents. Nothing builds solid relationships more than asking appropriate questions that honor the wisdom others possess. We hope that this book's collection of questions will help you navigate these challenges as you face ongoing and novel situations.

One of the questions found here in this book may be precisely what you need. Just as likely, one of these questions will trigger another question that fits your context even better. As you think about and experiment with these questions, you will become more skilled in developing and personalizing questions in your own words and finding unexpected opportunities to use questioning in a multitude of daily settings. Having an answer may be helpful, but having the right questions is where you will discover the most creative and innovative solutions.

Notes

1. As quoted in Gary B. Cohen, *Just Ask Leadership: Why Great Managers Always Ask the Right Questions* (New York: McGraw-Hill, 2009), 8.
2. As quoted in Al Gini and Ronald L. Green, *10 Virtues of Outstanding Leaders: Leadership and Character* (Hoboken, NJ: John Wiley & Sons, 2013).
3. As quoted in Andrew Young, *An Easy Burden* (New York: HarperCollins, 1996), 326.
4. For example: Karen Huang, Michael Yeomans, Alison Wood Brooks, Julia Minson, and Francesca Gino. "It Doesn't Hurt to Ask: Question-asking Increases Liking." *Journal of Personality and Social Psychology* 113, no. 3 September (2017): 430–452; and Alison Wood Brooks and

Francesca Gino, "Asking Advice Makes a Good Impression" in *SA Mind* Vol. 26 No. 2 (March 2015), 26. doi:https://doi.org/10.1038/scientificamericanmind0315-26.

5. Alan S. Berson and Richard G. Stieglitz, *Leadership Conversations: Challenging High-Potential Managers to Become Great Leaders* (San Francisco: Jossey-Bass, 2013), 180.
6. For example: Marilee G. Adams, *Change Your Questions, Change Your Life: 12 Powerful Tools for Leadership, Coaching, and Life*, 3rd ed. (Oakland, CA: Berrett-Koehler Publishers, 2016); Alison Wood Brooks and Leslie K. John, "The Surprising Power of Questions," *Harvard Business Review* 96, no. 2 (2018): 61–67; and John Hagel III, "Good Leadership Is About Asking Good Questions," *Harvard Business Review*, January 8, 2021, https://hbr.org/2021/01/good-leadership-is-about-asking-good-questions.
7. Jennifer Murtell, "The 5 Phases of Design Thinking," American Marketing Association. February 14, 2025. Accessed at https://www.ama.org/marketing-news/the-5-phases-of-design-thinking/; and Tim Brown, *Change by Design, Revised and Updated: How Design Thinking Transforms Organizations and Inspires Innovation* (New York: Harper Business, 2019).
8. Edgar H. Schein, *Humble Inquiry: The Gentle Art of Asking Instead of Telling* (Oakland, CA: Berrett-Koehler Publishers, 2013), 3–4.

2 Growing as a Leader

At a midsize marketing firm, Sarah had recently been promoted to team lead after consistently delivering high-quality campaigns. While confident in her technical skills, she knew that effective leadership required continuous growth and self-awareness. Eager to develop as a leader, Sarah took the initiative to schedule a one-on-one meeting with her manager, David, to explore how she could improve in her new role. During their conversation, Sarah came prepared with thoughtful questions that reflected her desire to develop her leadership abilities.

"What leadership qualities do you believe are most important in our organization?"

Sarah wanted to align her leadership style with the company's culture and expectations. This question helped her understand what traits were valued—such as adaptability, communication, and empathy—and how she could embody those in her daily work.

"Can you give me feedback on how I've handled team dynamics so far?"

Rather than waiting for formal reviews, Sarah sought real-time feedback. She asked David to highlight both her strengths and areas for improvement in managing interpersonal relationships, decision-making, and delegation.

"Who are some leaders within the company you think I could learn from?"

Sarah recognized the value of mentorship. By identifying experienced leaders, she could observe different leadership styles and potentially seek a mentor to guide her through challenges.

"What leadership development opportunities or training programs are available?"

Sarah was proactive in seeking formal growth opportunities. David informed her about upcoming workshops, cross-functional projects, and an internal leadership development program she could join.

By the end of the meeting, David was impressed by Sarah's initiative and reflective mindset. He noted that her questions demonstrated not only a desire for personal growth but also a deep understanding of the responsibilities of leadership. He recommended a mentor within the company, enrolled her in the next leadership workshop, and encouraged her to schedule monthly check-ins with him to track her progress.

★ ★ ★ ★ ★

Most of us don't start our lives as leaders; we learn about leadership from our experiences ("trial and error") and through the experiences of others. Some of our actions are effective, while others are not. We all make mistakes along the way. However, we develop our leadership capabilities by paying attention to what is happening and finding ways to learn from our experiences. We strive not to repeat the same mistakes, instead building on positive experiences from our cumulative undertakings.

Too often, leaders rely on the skills that brought them to their current positions, believing that if they were good enough to get them where they are, they will be sufficient for the future. Rarely is that the case. Leaders are always striving to become the best leader they hope to be.

Here's the rub: leadership can be learned; however, not everyone wants to, and not all those who do master leadership. Why? Because becoming the very best requires a strong belief in your ability to learn and grow, an intense aspiration to excel, the determination to challenge yourself, the recognition that you need the support of others, and the dedication to practice deliberately. Here are some questions to ask yourself on the journey to becoming a better leader.

Seeking Feedback

Questions

- Sheila Heen and Douglas Stone, both at Harvard Law School, study and write about how people can understand and improve how they receive feedback. As they point out, constructive feedback is the richest source of information for leadership development. If leaders do not invite such feedback, the only type they receive is unlikely to be constructive. It helps to avoid general requests such as "Do you have any feedback for me?" Heen and Stone suggest using more specific questions, such as:

   What's one thing you see me doing (or failing to do) that holds me back?[1]

- Marshall Goldsmith, an executive coach, well-known and regarded author, encourages leaders to seek regular feedback on their performance from a diverse range of people. He suggests that in soliciting personal feedback, the "only question that works" is:

   How can I do better?[2]

- Leadership coach Kristi Hedges developed a method for people to discover how they are perceived at work. After selecting five people who know your job well, all of whom you trust to give honest feedback, meet with each and ask them these questions:

    What's the general perception of me?

    What could I do differently that would have the greatest impact on my success?[3]

- Leadership scholars and award-winning authors Jim Kouzes and Barry Posner ask: "How can you know that you're doing what you say (which is the behavioral definition of credibility) if you never ask for feedback about your behavior? Asking for feedback gives you a perspective about yourself that only others can see. With this insight, you have the opportunity to make improvements."

    Publicly ask for feedback from others about how your actions affect them.[4]

- Sometimes leaders can dwell on their shortcomings and forget how important the things that they do well are. Another way to improve is to analyze your strengths and then ask yourself this question:

    What is something I do exceptionally well that may help me address a weakness that I have?

- Leaders find it helpful to reflect on the strength of their connections with those with whom they work. Questions that can help in this analysis might be:

What parts of my team, organization, etc., know me best?

What parts know me least?

What parts do I know best?

What parts do I know least?

Legacy

Questions

- Shortly before she left the presidency of the Girl Scouts of the USA, Frances Hesselbein was interviewed at a seminar by Peter Drucker. His question may help you or others think about one's life purpose:

    When you have left this organization and
    they hang your portrait on the wall,
    what do you hope the brass plaque beneath
    your portrait will say about you?

- Thinking about legacies requires leaders to move beyond short-term definitions of success because they encompass the past, present, and future. Reflecting on them prompts you to consider where you've been, where you are now, and where you are going, bringing you face-to-face with questions about who you are and why you are here. Ask yourself:

    What is the difference I want to make?

    Why is it essential to be moving in that direction,
    and for those who come after me who will inherit
    what I leave?[5]

- Leaders are often tempted to think about what they might do in a future position. Some high-potential leaders struggle rather than grow because they fail to invest fully in the work they are currently doing. This is part of the "talent curse" described by INSEAD Professors Jennifer and Gianpiero Petriglieri, who offer perspective with this question:

> *What if my current job is not a stepping stone but a destination?*[6]

- When you are offered a leadership role, either as a volunteer or as an employee, questions that might help you decide to accept or decline the opportunity include:

> *Do I care about this work (product, service, client, etc.)?*
>
> *Is this opportunity congruent with my mission, values, and goals?*
>
> *Will I find meaning in doing the tasks involved with this position?*
>
> *Do I want to work with the people associated with this role?*

Self-Evaluation

Questions

- Psychologist Howard Gardner asks a question that is applicable in various contexts. He says that a person with an ethical mind asks:

> *If all workers in my profession . . . did what I do, what would the world be like?*[7]

- When taking on a leadership position, questions that might help you prepare for the new responsibilities include:

    What new competencies will I need for this new role?

    How will I gain these new skills?

    What prior experiences can I draw on that are most similar to the new challenge?

    Whom can I ask to be a mentor?

- It's easy to get offended when things are said about people that are not true. This is understandable. Yet, when this happens, it might be a time to reflect on why such things are being said. In such a situation, a coach or counselor will often ask this question:

    What would lead someone to think such a thing about you?

- Honest self-evaluation can be difficult. Questions such as these may make this easier:

    If I were my supervisor, how would I describe myself?

    If someone asked those with whom I work to describe me, what would they say about me?

- W. Edwards Deming, perhaps the most prominent name associated with the "quality" movement, says that there are three crucial questions that 80% of people cannot answer with any measure of confidence. How would you respond to these questions?

    What is my job?

    What in it really counts?

    How well am I doing?

Reflection

Questions

- After a difficult meeting or conversation, it sometimes helps to take a few minutes before moving on to the next thing to reflect by asking yourself:

  Did I handle this situation well?

  What could I have done differently?

  What can I learn from this experience to help me in the future?

- All leaders are busy. There never seems to be time for planning or looking ahead. The challenges of each day can easily overwhelm leaders. Technology futurist Daniel Burrus suggests that at such times, leaders stop for a moment and reflect on this question:

  In order to speed up, what am I willing to slow down?[8]

- In all groups, people will make mistakes. Entrepreneur and consultant Eric Ries encourages groups to adopt two simple rules. The first is to be tolerant of all mistakes the first time, and the second is to never allow the same mistake to be made twice. An invaluable personal question for you whenever something goes wrong would be:

  How could I prevent myself from being in this situation ever again?[9]

- Researchers have demonstrated the power of experience in helping leaders grow. However, simply having various experiences is not enough. Growth depends on learning from those experiences. Thought Leadership Lab CEO Denise Brosseau suggests these questions to use after a project, job, event, or assignment that can help make learning more likely:

What have I learned from this experience?

What did I do well?

What could I have done differently?

Is there a universal lesson here that others could apply?[10]

Continuing to Grow

Questions

- All leaders need to continue learning and growing. This is especially true when faced with new opportunities, challenges, or technologies. At such times, ask these questions:

  What is something about which I need to learn more?

  Who can suggest sources?

  Where can I begin that learning?

- Leaders are always looking for ways to improve. That is how good leaders become great leaders. One simple question to ask repeatedly is:

  What is one current behavior that, if I could change it, would make a significant and positive difference in the quality of my leadership?

- Many leaders, especially those at or near the top of leadership in their organizations, find that they are often insulated from the kinds of critical feedback or clues that previously they relied upon to shape their planning and actions. Hal Gregersen, executive director of MIT's Leadership Center, suggests leaders who think they may be in this situation should ask themselves:

> *How many barriers do people have to cross to talk directly with me?*
>
> *How much of my typical workweek is spent outside my office or organization?*
>
> *How many questions do I ask versus statements I make in typical conversations?*
>
> *How many times this week have I said, "I don't know," in response to a question?*[11]

Notes

1. Sheila Heen and Douglas Stone, "Find the Coaching in Criticism," *Harvard Business Review*, Vol. 92, Issue 1 (January–February 2014), 111.
2. Marshall Goldsmith, *What Got You Here Won't Get You There* (New York: Hyperion, 2007), 122.
3. Kristi Hedges, "How Are You Perceived at Work? Here's an Exercise to Find Out," published on hbr.org, December 19, 2017, https://hbr.org/2017/12/how-are-you-perceived-at-work-heres-an-exercise-to-find-out.
4. James M. Kouzes and Barry Z. Posner, *The Leadership Challenge: How to Make Extraordinary Things Happen in Organizations*, 6th Ed. (Hoboken, NJ: John Wiley & Sons, 2017), 82, 92.
5. James M. Kouzes and Barry Z. Posner, *A Leader's Legacy* (Hoboken, NJ: John Wiley & Sons, 2006), 175.
6. Jennifer Petriglieri and Gianpiero Petriglieri, "The Talent Curse: Why High Potentials Struggle – And How They Can Grow through It," *Harvard Business Review*, Vol. 95, Issue 3 (May–June 2017), 94.

7. "The Ethical Mind: A Conversation with Psychologist Howard Gardner," *Harvard Business Review*, Vol. 85, Issue 3 (March 2007), 52.
8. Daniel Burrus, *Flash Foresight: How to See the Invisible and Do the Impossible* (New York: Harper Business, 2011), 46.
9. Eric Ries, *The Lean Startup* (New York: Crown Business, 2011), 236–237.
10. Denise Brosseau, *Ready to Be a Thought Leader? How to Increase Your Influence, Impact, and Success* (San Francisco: Jossey-Bass, 2013), 129.
11. Hal Gregersen, "Bursting the CEO Bubble: Why Executives Should Talk Less and Ask More Questions," *Harvard Business Review*, Vol. 95, No. 2 (March–April 2017), 81.

3 | Facing Challenges

Maria is a plant operations manager at a manufacturing firm facing a major production bottleneck due to outdated machinery and an over-complicated workflow. The delays are hurting delivery times and customer satisfaction. Leadership has tasked her with turning operations around within six months. To lead through this challenge, Maria knows she must ask the right questions across multiple dimensions.

1. **Getting Started: What's the core challenge we need to solve?**

    Maria begins by asking, "What's not working, and why?" She organizes cross-functional meetings with frontline workers, engineers, and shift supervisors to pinpoint key causes of the bottleneck—outdated machines, unclear procedures, and lack of ownership over quality control.

2. **Identifying Resources: What do we already have, and what do we need?**

    She conducts a gap analysis: "Do we have the budget, skills, and personnel to execute the fix?" She identifies underused team expertise and negotiates with finance for funds to rent temporary machinery during the upgrade.

3. **Connecting to Purpose: How does solving this problem align with our mission?**

    Maria reinforces that this isn't just about production numbers—it's about delivering reliable, quality products to customers who depend on them. She reminds the team that improved performance directly supports jobs, customer trust, and company growth.

4. **Monitoring Progress: How will we measure our progress?**

    She implements daily stand-up meetings and a dashboard to track key metrics like production output, downtime, and defect rates. These indicators give her real-time insight into whether changes are working.

5. **Evaluating Performance: Are our changes making a measurable difference?**

    After the first month, Maria reviews whether production speed and quality have improved. She asks, "Where are we gaining? Where are we still stuck?" The team uses this data to recalibrate actions.

6. **Fostering Learning: What are we discovering, and how can we share it?**

    She encourages team members to share lessons learned, both successes and setbacks, in weekly huddles. These insights help other teams avoid repeated mistakes and foster a culture of continuous improvement.

7. **Creative Abandonment: What should we stop doing?**

    Maria challenges long-held practices, asking, "What processes no longer serve us?" One example is eliminating an outdated double-signoff procedure that caused delays with no added value.

By asking thoughtful, strategic questions, Maria leads her team not just to fix a problem but to evolve. The result is more efficient operations, empowered employees, and a model for navigating future challenges with purpose and adaptability.

★ ★ ★ ★ ★

Challenge is the domain of leaders and what stands between the current reality and successfully achieving the organization's mission and goals. Managers handle the status quo, and it is leaders like Maria who take people and organizations to places they have never been before.

Researchers who studied thousands of personal-best leadership experiences concluded that challenge was the common denominator of the context in which people said they did their very best: "Challenge is the crucible for leadership and the opportunity for greatness. Challenge shapes us, and challenge opens doors."[1]

To say we live in challenging times would be an understatement. The presence of challenges and problems is a given. The choice confronting leaders is how to handle them.

Getting Started

Questions

- Leadership consultant Margaret Wheatley says that when one faces a problem, it does not help to ask, "What went wrong?" That simply makes people angry. The better question she learned to ask was:

    What's possible and who cares?

- Wheatley goes on to indicate how leaders often let problems become burdens that wear them down. She suggests a sequence of questions, which ensures that a group, and not just the leader, is engaging its problems and future:

    What is the system where there is a problem?

    Who has a stake in that system?

    Do they understand they are a part of the system with a problem?

> *Which people can come together to remember that they all share in this issue?*
>
> *How can they share information and work together on ways to address the issue?*[2]

- Often in a meeting, leaders are reminded of a looming challenge or opportunity. To test with the group the urgency of the issue, you might ask:

    > *Are there steps we should be taking now to prepare for this eventuality?*

- People often move too quickly to solving problems, according to consultants Keith Michaelson and Markus Spiegel. They suggest a series of questions that can transform problem-solving into shaping challenges:

    > *What problem are we trying to solve?*
    >
    > *Why is it important to solve this problem?*
    >
    > *What would success look like?*
    >
    > *What would be a challenging but achievable near-term result?*[3]

- When a leader must address a significant problem, the challenge can seem overwhelming. Questions like these can help you sort the issues into more manageable units:

    > *What can I do in the short term?*
    >
    > *What can I do over a longer term?*

What parts of the problem are in my control, and what parts are not?

What are my options, and what are the advantages and disadvantages of each?

Thinking Outside the Box

Questions

- Research finds that the effectiveness rating of leaders is directly proportional to the extent that their direct reports observe them actively searching for innovative ways to improve.[4] Even if you're on the right track, you are likely to be run over if you sit there. Here are some helpful questions for challenging assumptions:

  What if the opposite of what we believe is true?

  Are we doing this because it works, or because it's the way it's always been done?

  What assumptions are we making, and what happens if we challenge them?

  What ideas would we try if we weren't afraid of failing?

- Another way to get yourself and others thinking outside of the box is to imagine alternatives, not taking any existing practice as set in stone. For example, ask:

  If budget, time, or resources weren't an issue, how would we solve this?

  How would someone from a completely different industry approach this?

  What would we do if we had to deliver this solution in 24 hours?

- Pushing the boundaries around existing thinking, paradigms, processes, and experiences is another way a leader challenges people to imagine the possibilities. You could ask:

  What's one bold move we've never considered—but maybe should?

  How can we achieve a 10x improvement, rather than just a 10% increase?

  What rule would we break (or rewrite) to make this better?

  What's the most unconventional solution we can think of?

- Leadership scholars Jim Kouzes and Barry Posner encourage leaders to exercise "outsight" (the awareness and understanding of outside forces), which they refer to as the sibling of insight (the ability to comprehend the inner nature of things). That's because researchers have found that innovations can come from almost anywhere, including a global study of CEOs who indicated that the most significant sources of innovative ideas are discovered outside their organization.[5] Make it a habit always to be looking around and asking not just for yourself but also for those around you:

  What's new?

  What's next?

  What's better?[6]

- One manager we interviewed is known for being very curious about what's going on around her and for "always asking questions." One of her direct reports described her as being "unrelenting in her questions until she completely understands whatever is being discussed." In looking outside of her experience, she broadens her perspective. Questions such as these can do the same for you and others:

Who else could we involve to bring fresh insights?

What's happening in other industries or cultures that we could learn from?

Are we limiting ourselves by thinking too narrowly?

- There is a powerful impulse when confronted with a problem to "solve it." Research shows that leaders and their teams devote too little time and effort to examining and defining the problem before beginning to resolve it. To avoid this trap, IMD Professors Julia Binder and Michael Watkins, suggest reframing the issue by asking questions such as:

    Are we solving the right problem—or just the most obvious one?

    If we reframed this as an opportunity instead of a problem, what would change?

    What would happen if we viewed this from the customer's perspective?

    What would a child (or someone with no experience in our field) suggest?[7]

Identifying Resources

Questions

- Sam Walton, the legendary founder of Walmart, was a remarkably successful businessperson who started small and built a giant retail enterprise during his lifetime. He was known for learning from others, including competitors. One question that served him well might also be valuable for you to consider pondering:

Who else has or is struggling with a similar problem, and what can I learn from them?[8]

- Leaders often face a crisis or problem and think that nothing like this has happened before. Even when a situation appears utterly different from anything that has come before, you need to view what's happening in the context of history. You need to understand what others have done when faced with similar adverse circumstances. Leadership scholars Jim Kouzes and Barry Posner suggest that you must "broaden the context" when turning adversity into an opportunity. They suggest asking yourself and other people you are working with these questions:

What's the bigger picture here?

How can we help people understand what's happening in the broader environment and how it is affecting the business?

How can we educate others about the larger context?

How can we get people to see that we're not any worse off than others were before us?

How can we provide people with the time and space to discuss their answers and gain a broader perspective?

What can we do to frame what is happening and being done in ways that give people hope?[9]

- One characteristic of adaptive challenges (as opposed to technical difficulties) is that an adaptive issue always requires people to learn more about the situation. In light of this need, this question may help frame your thinking:

   What are the gaps in our knowledge of this issue for which we need to learn more?

- The next time you and those with whom you work are facing a particularly challenging dilemma, you might try posing the following question to the group. Seeking a solution through such a question can strengthen a group of people. It affirms that the leader has faith in the team's ability to work together and devise a solution.

   This is a truly big problem. What do you think we need to know and do to solve it?

Connecting to Purpose

Questions

- Best-selling author and consultant Simon Sinek has helped many leaders by reminding them that an organization's first focus should not be on "what we do" or "how we do it" but rather on "*why* we do it." In light of that emphasis, he suggests this is the right question to be asking:

   WHY did we start doing WHAT we are doing in the first place?[10]

- Don Frick's biography of Robert Greenleaf, the individual most often associated with the concept of "servant leadership," reports that Greenleaf believed there were two questions that needed to be asked much more often by individuals and organizations:

  > *What are you trying to do?*
  >
  > *Whom do you serve?*[11]

- Ensuring that all events and special programs are reviewed each time they occur is a crucial responsibility for leaders. Here are possible questions to use for this reflection:

  > *Did we have a clear purpose for this event*
  > *(we will do x so that y happens)?*
  >
  > *In what ways did the event contribute to advancing our overall mission?*
  >
  > *Did we achieve our goal?*
  >
  > *To the extent that we did not, what did we learn that will help in the future?*
  >
  > *Would there be a more effective way to achieve the goal we sought?*

- Most organizations tend to add new events and activities without eliminating other current programs. It can help to encourage groups planning for the coming year to ask questions about each of their programs:

  > *Why do we do this?*
  >
  > *Do we regularly achieve the intended purpose?*
  >
  > *Are the results enough to justify the time, energy, and resources expended?*

Monitoring Progress

Questions

- Many leaders experience planning processes that are soon forgotten, including all the grand goals that are set. One way to keep leaders accountable to all the people who invested hours in developing those plans is to build in monthly or bi-monthly reviews of progress. Here are possible questions:

    What has been completed so far?

    What is on schedule for completion?

    What is lagging?

    Who is resisting?

    What can we do?

- When leaders find themselves during an effort with others in which everyone is frustrated by a lack of progress, sometimes it helps to regroup with questions such as:

    Where are we now?

    Where do we need to be?

    What do we need to do to achieve this goal?

Evaluating Performance

Questions

- Evaluating a program or project is crucial and demanding. Posing these questions at the beginning of the process can be helpful:

> *What is the purpose of what we are assessing?*
>
> *What questions are we trying to answer?*
>
> *What information will we need, and how will we get it?*
>
> *Is our evaluation plan logical, realistic, and practical?*

- After any significant event, Margaret Wheatley strongly recommends participants should take the time to discuss what happened. She offers these three simple questions:

  > *What happened?*
  >
  > *Why do we think it happened?*
  >
  > *What can we learn from it?*[12]

- Peter Drucker, the influential management thinker, says that an organization should regularly raise the following question about every activity and program:

  > *If we hadn't done this already, knowing what we now know, would we start it?*

- Despite the best intentions and hard work, some efforts simply do not work out as leaders hoped they would. When an undertaking fails to achieve its goals, a typical response is to affix blame. A more valuable and practical approach is to ask questions, such as:

  > *What did we learn from this experience?*
  >
  > *What does this say about our assumptions and approach?*
  >
  > *What have we learned to do differently next time?*

- Evaluation is an excellent way to make good things better. Here are three simple questions to use after any undertaking:

    What did we do right?

    What did we do wrong?

    What else should we have done?

Fostering Learning

Questions

- Explore these questions when you sense or observe that participation and energy levels are varying considerably among activities or programs:

    What programs thrive without extraordinary promotion and encouragement?

    What programs struggle no matter what we do?

    What can we learn from existing programs as we begin new ones?

- If a leader has questions or uneasiness about the effectiveness of a program or initiative, it may be easier to open the topic in a less direct manner than criticism. One way you can start such conversations might be:

    What do you know about . . . ?

    Could you explain more about . . . ?

- Few organizations are as skilled as they need to be in adapting to changing circumstances. These three questions are used by Johnson & Johnson as they develop plans for each of their business units:

> *What has changed?*
>
> *Why?*
>
> *What are we going to do about it?*[13]

- Imposing or even offering your help to a group to improve something in which they are highly invested runs the risk of communicating unintended criticism or judgment. Renowned organizational development consultants and authors Judith Katz and Frederick Miller suggest the following question may reduce their resistance:

> *How can we make this work even better?*[14]

Creative Abandonment

Questions

- Amid limited time, energy, and resources, organizations that continue to add new activities while maintaining all their current ones quickly find themselves overextended. It is challenging to gain momentum in any strategic direction because a significant amount of energy is expended on numerous disparate initiatives without a carefully coordinated focus. The tendency to continue efforts that are not fruitful might be avoided by asking this question:

> *Are there things we are trying to do better that we should no longer be doing at all?*

- One organization found a way for various components to save money and time by asking each to build in regular evaluation that included this question:

   What is one thing that, if it were eliminated, would not affect the quality of your work?

- Many people find it helpful to ask, "If we didn't already have this, would we start it?" of any program, activity, or position. Another version of this line of inquiry addresses the costs and benefits of an undertaking:

   If we were not already doing this,
   how much time and money would we spend to start it?

- Testing a new idea using a short-term pilot is one prudent way to experiment, and companies run these all the time. "Reverse pilots" focus on testing the removal of an initiative or process. The goal is not necessarily to improve results, but to decrease complexity without making things worse in the short term. Experiment with a short-term break in an existing program to see if they are missed and by how much. The right question to ask in these instances, according to LinkedIn's COO Daniel Shapero is:

   What things might we pause for a brief moment to observe what happens?

   What could be dismantled, scaled back or sun-setted without serious consequences?[15]

Testing Routines

Questions

- Periodically but regularly, put this question on your staff or team's agenda, inviting each person to bring their best answers. Then the total group would discuss and select one of the options. The question is:

   > *What rule, form, or procedure no longer serves a purpose?*

- Time is a challenge for all leaders. At least every six months, it is prudent to ask yourself these questions:

   > *What am I doing that could or even should be done by someone else?*
   >
   > *What am I doing that does not need to be done by me or even anyone else?*

- At least annually, guide your team or organization in asking questions that can, over the coming months, free up valuable time for new initiatives. Lisa Bodell, a global leader on simplification, collaboration, and innovation, offers these questions:

   > *Are there things we do that add no value?*
   >
   > *Are there reports we can do without?*
   >
   > *What recurring meetings can be held less frequently?*
   >
   > *Are there meetings that are not needed?*
   >
   > *What presentations can be shortened?*
   >
   > *Can approvals be simplified?*
   >
   > *Can we eliminate any forms or documents?*[16]

- Any group that works together for a time might refresh and better align themselves, according to management consultants Robert Bruce Shaw and Mark Ronald, by occasionally asking:

Are there things that we do that no longer make any sense? Why do we do them?[17]

Notes

1. James M. Kouzes and Barry Z. Posner, *The Leadership Challenge: How to Make Extraordinary Things Happen in Organizations*, 7th ed (Hoboken, NJ: John Wiley & Sons, 2023), xix.
2. Elizabeth Donohoe Steinberger, "Margaret Wheatley on Leadership and Change," *School Administrator*, Vol. 52, No. 1 (January 1, 1995), 16–20.
3. Keith Michaelson and Markus Spiegel, "Stop Solving Your Business Problems," *Leader to Leader*, Vol. 56 (Spring, 2010), 57–60.
4. James M. Kouzes and Barry Z. Posner, *op. cit.*, 148.
5. See, for example, John E. Ettlie, *Managing Innovation*, 2nd ed. (Abingdon, UK: Taylor & Francis, 2006); Steven Johnson, *Where Good Ideas Come From: The Natural History of Innovation* (New York: Riverhead, 2010); Eric Ries, *The Lean Startup: How Constant Innovation Creates Radically Successful Businesses* (New York: Penguin Group, 2011); Tony Davila, Marc Epstein, and Robert Shelton, *Making Innovation Work: How to Manage It, Measure It, and Profit from It*, rev. ed. (Upper Saddle River, NJ: FT Press, 2012); Isaac Asimov, "How Do People Get New Ideas?" *MIT Technology Review*, October 20, 2014, https://www.technologyreview.com/s/531911/isaac-asimov-asks-how-do-people-get-new-ideas/, accessed June 30, 2025; and IBM, "Expanding the Innovation Horizons: The Global CEO Study" 2006 (Somers, NY: IBM Global Services, 2006).
6. James M. Kouzes and Barry Z. Posner, *op. cit.*, 168.
7. Julia Binder and Michael D. Watkins, "To Solve a Tough Problem, Reframe It," *Harvard Business Review*, Vol. 102, Issue 1 (January–February 2024), 80–89.
8. Chip Heath and Dan Heath, *Decisive: How to Make Better Choices in Life and Work* (New York: Crown Business, 2013), 69.

9. James M. Kouzes and Barry Z. Posner, *Turning Adversity into Opportunity* (Hoboken, NJ: John Wiley & Sons, 2014), 8–9.
10. Simon Sinek, *Start with Why: How Great Leaders Inspire Everyone to Take Action* (New York: Penguin, 2009), 51.
11. Don M. Frick, *Robert K. Greenleaf: A Life of Servant Leadership* (Oakland, CA: Berrett-Koehler Publishers, 2004), 253.
12. Margaret Wheatley, *Leadership and the New Science: Discovering Order in a Chaotic World*, (Oakland, CA: Berrett-Koehler Publishers, 1992).
13. Jay W. Lorsch and Rakesh Khurana, with Philip Caldwell, George D. Kennedy, G. G. Michelson, Henry Wendt, and Alfred M. Zeien, "Changing Leaders: The Board's Role in CEO Succession," *Harvard Business Review*, Vol. 77, Issue 3 (May–June 1999), 94.
14. Judith H. Katz and Frederick A. Miller, "Judging Others Has Not Worked . . . So Let's Join Them," *Leader to Leader*, Vol. 70 (Fall, 2013), 55–60.
15. Daniel Shapero, "Great Managers Prune as Well as Plant," LinkedIn (December 13, 2012), https://www.linkedin.com/pulse/20121213073143-314058-great-managers-prune-as-well-as-plant.
16. Lisa Bodell, *Why Simple Wins* (Brookline, MA: Bibliomotion, 2017), 165.
17. Robert B. Shaw and Mark Ronald, "Changing Culture – Patience is Not a Virtue," *Leader to Leader*, Vol. 66 (Fall, 2012), 51–56.

4 | Leading Change

Jeremy, director of student services at a large university, is leading a major initiative to digitize all academic advising and support services. The goal is to create a more accessible and student-centered experience. However, the change requires rethinking long-standing processes, retraining staff, and shifting a deeply rooted culture built around in-person interactions.

To lead this transition effectively, Jeremy begins by asking questions critical to leading change.

1. **Understanding Organizational Culture: What values and beliefs shape how we currently operate?**

    Jeremy asks himself and his team, "What do we pride ourselves on, and what are we hesitant to give up?" He discovers a strong culture of personal connection and hands-on support. Recognizing this, he frames the change not as a replacement but as an enhancement of personalized service.

2. **Planning: What outcomes are we aiming for, and how will we get there?**

    He defines clear goals—reducing wait times, increasing student satisfaction, and improving access for remote learners. He then maps out timelines, responsibilities, and communication strategies to keep the team aligned.

3. **Assessing Opportunities and Challenges: Where are the risks, and where can we create value?**

   Jeremy conducts a SWOT analysis with his leadership team. Opportunities include expanding reach and increasing efficiency; challenges involve staff resistance, training needs, and technology reliability.

4. **What-If Scenarios: What could go wrong, and how can we prepare for it?**

   He explores potential pitfalls: "What if the system crashes during peak enrollment?" or "What if staff morale drops?" He builds contingency plans, including manual backup systems and wellness check-ins for staff during the rollout.

5. **Focusing: What matters most right now?**

   To avoid feelings of being overwhelmed, Jeremy prioritizes one service area for the initial launch—academic advising—before expanding to others. He reminds the team to focus on what students need most: timely, accurate, and empathetic support.

6. **Learning: How will we gather feedback and adapt as we go?**

   He sets up feedback loops, including student surveys, focus groups, and weekly team debriefs. These learning mechanisms allow for agile improvements and demonstrate a commitment to collaboration and continuous improvement.

By asking these questions, Jeremy leads change not as a top-down mandate but as a shared journey rooted in culture, strategic planning, and thoughtful learning. The result is not just a digital system but a more adaptive, responsive student services team.

★ ★ ★ ★ ★

Change is the work of leaders. In today's world, business-as-usual thinking is unacceptable, and leaders know that they must transform the way things are being done. Delivering results beyond expectations can't be achieved with good intentions. People, processes, systems, and strategies all need to change. In addition, all change requires that leaders actively seek ways to make things better—to grow, innovate, and improve. There's a clear relationship between challenge and change, and there's a clear connection between challenge and being an effective leader.

This perspective is consistent with what researchers have found in examining the human resource practices and organizational designs of innovation-producing organizations, as they seek to learn both what fosters and what hinders innovation in corporations. Innovation means change, and "change requires leadership . . . a 'prime mover' to push for implementation of strategic decisions."[1] Leadership is inextricably linked to the process of innovation, which involves experimenting and introducing new ideas.

While, like the best leaders, you need to recognize that the past and the present can inform and inspire, the future is also the realm where you need to focus your attention. Handled well, change can be seen as writing the next chapter of a story that began before your time and should last far longer than any current participants.

Understanding Your Organization's Identity

Questions

- The culture or DNA of every organization is unique. An organization's identity takes shape early, just as a newborn child develops their distinguishing features. As time passes, the identity becomes more pronounced. Not everything in that identity is ideal any more than each life is perfect. You must have an understanding and appreciation of the culture because change and growth will flow more naturally and effectively when they emerge from this identity. This question causes people to think, but also elicits essential clues about an organization:

    If you had to describe our organization (company) in one word, what would it be?

- Psychologist and business theorist Ed Schein suggested that you needed to ask questions about the organization's values, norms, history, and how people interact in order to uncover the "shared basic assumptions" that formed the basis of an organization's identity:

> *Why does our organization exist, beyond just making a profit?*
>
> *What is the one thing we consistently strive to achieve that defines our ultimate contribution?*
>
> *What are the official values of our organization? Which of these values are truly lived out in daily decisions and behaviors?*
>
> *What are the key stories or turning points in our organization's history that shaped who we are today?*
>
> *What do we do better than almost anyone else?*
>
> *How do people typically interact with each other here?*
>
> *What aspects of our current identity do we absolutely want to preserve as we grow or change?*[2]

- This is a question you can check in with both yourself and others, and it can be modified for use in many settings and circumstances:

> *What makes me (or us) most proud about being a part of this organization?*

- Seeking to understand how they were perceived in their community (or marketplace), a regional healthcare organization developed an online survey. They asked a relevant sample of people these questions:

When you hear [organization's name], what word, phrase, or image first comes to mind?

If someone asked you what you know about [organization's name], what is one thing you would say?

If someone asked you what the people who work at [organization's name] are like, what would you tell them?

Planning for Change

Questions

- Planning never seems so important as when the results of poor planning become obvious. Leaders understand the need to plan and to build a planning culture within their organizations. Good intentions and trusting that everyone knows what to do will not suffice. Planning allows drawing from the collective wisdom of many—especially those needed to carry out the plans—when not under the pressure of implementing immediate tasks. Planning takes time, but generally, when all is said and done, it saves time. For example, organizations develop new programs, services, or products to meet emerging needs or changing circumstances. Accordingly, a valuable question to ask at least annually is:

    What is the emerging trend or need that we should give attention to in the coming year?

- The focus of strategic planning is to anticipate and adjust for changes expected in the future. However, to balance this perspective, you might also address this question, which is too often neglected:

    What is not going to change in the next five to ten years?

- Lisa Bodell, an expert on simplifying organizational processes, believes these questions help leaders get at the heart of assessing the merits of a project:

> *Is it valuable? (worth the time)*
>
> *Is it minimal? (streamlined)*
>
> *Is it understandable? (clear)*
>
> *Is it repeatable? (model for other things)*
>
> *Is it accessible? (readily available)*[3]

Opportunities and Challenges

Questions

- In planning for the future, many organizations find it helpful to ask these questions:

> *What current strengths do we possess that we can utilize to address the opportunities and challenges we face?*
>
> *What new skills or competencies do we need to develop to meet the opportunities and challenges we face?*

- When organizations plan for the future, a good balance of attention to opportunities and challenges is essential. That is, avoid opportunity blindness and risk ignorance. Rather than adopting a purely optimistic or pessimistic view, advocate for a holistic and realistic assessment of the external landscape and internal capabilities by asking such questions as:

> *What unmet or underserved needs do our current or potential customers have that we are uniquely positioned to address?*

What emerging technologies, demographic shifts, or lifestyle changes could create entirely new markets or demands for us?

Where are our competitors not focusing that could be a significant whitespace for us?

What are the most significant threats from new competitors, disruptive technologies, or changing regulations?

What "black swan" event (highly improbable, high-impact) should we consider, even if unlikely, to build resilience?

Are there any shifts in consumer behavior, economic conditions, or political stability that could severely impact our operations or demand?

Where are we most vulnerable (i.e., any areas that, if not addressed soon, could seriously undermine our mission)?

- Knowing how easy it is for any group to spread its efforts and resources so broadly as to have minimal impact, this is how one organization uses the following question as a guide for its annual program and budget planning:

    In what area do we have enough energy, leadership, and potential that, if we concentrated our efforts and resources there in the coming year, we could advance that part of our work to a new level of excellence?

- When preparing to launch a new venture, serial entrepreneurs Steve Blank and Bob Dorf, suggest considering deeply your responses to these two questions before moving forward:

  What one thing must happen for this effort to succeed?

  What one thing must not happen for this effort to succeed?[4]

- Many people struggle with finding a balance between being supportive and feeling overwhelmed. Elizabeth Lotardo, a fellow at the Institute of Coaching, suggests you empower your team to think and act for themselves by asking these questions:

  What have you tried?

  What or who is getting in the way?

  What support do you need?

  What would you do if you were in my seat?

  Is there anything else I should be aware of?[5]

What If?

Questions

- "What-if" questions are incredibly useful for leading change for many reasons. For one, they promote future-oriented thinking and visioning by compelling individuals and groups to look beyond the current state and imagine different possible futures, both positive and negative. This helps to clarify the desired outcome of the change and build a compelling vision. For example:

  Imagine we are five years from now, and we've been incredibly successful.

> *What specific results have we achieved that make us proudest?*
>
> *What does our ideal customer/client experience look like in the future?*
>
> *If our organization were featured in a leading business publication five years from now, what would the headline say about our greatest accomplishment?*

- The following questions, suggests Woody Wade, a scenario planning expert, aim to uncover hidden beliefs, question established ways of doing things, and open doors to new possibilities:

  > *What assumptions are we currently making about our customers/market/technology that might no longer be true?*
  >
  > *What deeply held beliefs do we have about "how things work around here" that might be limiting us?*
  >
  > *If we stopped doing [specific activity/process] entirely, what would happen? What would be the consequences, good or bad?*
  >
  > *What are we doing today that, if we were starting fresh, we would never do?*
  >
  > *If a new competitor entered the market with unlimited resources, how would they disrupt our current way of operating?*[6]

- When freed from the constraints of the present, people are more likely to brainstorm novel solutions and approaches to challenges, leading to more innovative change strategies. Paul Shoemaker, founding president of Social Venture Partners International, points out that scenario planning is key to strategic thinking. By asking these types of "what-if" questions, you can unlock fresh perspectives, encourage divergent thinking, and foster an environment where unconventional ideas are not only welcomed but actively sought out:

   What if we had no budget at all for this project? Or an unlimited budget? How would we achieve our goal?

   What if our most demanding customer was on our design team? What changes would they insist on?

   What if we were a tech startup trying to disrupt our own industry? How would we approach this problem?

   What if this solution had to be usable by a 5-year-old (or an 80-year-old)? How would we simplify it?

   What if we removed the most obvious feature/step of our current solution? How else could we achieve the outcome?

   What if we aimed to make this process delightfully inefficient (to learn what's truly essential)?

   What if a primary resource for this project disappeared or customer needs drastically changed overnight due to [global event/new trend]? How would we adapt?[7]

- To build buy-in and reduce resistance to change, questions should be designed to involve people in exploring the change, addressing their concerns, highlighting benefits, and demonstrating how the change aligns with their interests. The goal is to move from a place of fear or skepticism to one of understanding and ownership. Here are some possible what-if questions to consider for this purpose:

What if we continue with the status quo? What persistent problems or frustrations will remain unsolved?

What if this change works even better than we expect? What positive ripple effects could it have for our daily work, our clients, or our personal development?

What if there are unexpected challenges during the transition? How can we best support each other and adapt?

What if someone struggles to adapt to the new way? What kind of support or training would be most helpful for them?

What if we tapped into the unique expertise of everyone on this team to implement this change? What specific contributions could you then envision yourself making?

What if this change ultimately leads to [more meaningful work, less frustration, greater recognition] for you personally? How would that feel?

- When leaders are involved in planning a new initiative or event, there is excitement about getting it started. It is good to remember that, as Wharton Professor Terry Fadem noted, while you may have a good sense of your hopes and dreams, you usually cannot know how others will receive them. Questions to consider along the way that can help prepare for the eventual results include:

    What if this does not work?

    What if it works far better than we expect?[28]

- In assessing the potential outcomes of a proposed effort, be sure to ask those involved in the planning for their thoughts on these what-if type questions:

  What would be the ideal outcome?

  What would be a good outcome?

  What would be a terrible outcome?

Focusing

Questions

- In leading change, focus is absolutely critical because change initiatives are inherently complex, often disruptive, and can easily lose momentum or veer off course without a clear, unwavering direction. These questions help keep everyone on track:

  What is the single most critical outcome we absolutely must achieve with this change initiative?

  Why are we undertaking this change now?

  What is the core problem we are trying to solve, or the key opportunity we are trying to seize, through this change?

  What does "success" for this change look like, specifically, and how will we measure it?

- Maintaining focus and prioritization are critical in any change (leadership) initiative. You can help ensure this happening, according to Harvard Business School Professor John Kotter, by asking questions like:

Is this activity/task directly contributing to our core change outcome? If not, why are we doing it?

What is the highest-leverage activity we could be working on right now to move this change forward?

What new information or challenges have emerged that might require us to re-evaluate our focus, or can we absorb it without derailing?

What's one thing we could stop doing that would free up energy and focus for this change?[9]

- Eliminating distractions is incredibly helpful for focusing, as doing so creates an optimal environment for getting our brains to perform at their best. It's about consciously creating conditions that allow for deep concentration, leading to improved performance, reduced stress, and ultimately, greater success in your endeavors. These questions pave the way for being able to focus more effectively:

    What is currently taking my attention away from my most important work?

    What obstacles or roadblocks am I encountering that are preventing me from focusing?

    Are there any tasks I'm doing that could be delegated or eliminated?

    Where am I spending my time and energy that isn't aligned with my top priorities?

- Think about what you can do to help clarify priorities and address distractions for the people you are working with. Asking the right questions can empower individuals to identify their own obstacles and develop strategies for greater concentration:

   What is the most critical thing you need to accomplish today/this week?

   How does this task/project directly contribute to our team's/organization's goals?

   What are the most significant external distractions you're currently facing (e.g., constant notifications, noisy environment, frequent interruptions)?

   How are you currently managing those distractions?

   What support do you need from me or the team to reduce these interruptions?

Learning Agenda

Questions

- Having a learning agenda for leading change is a proactive and strategic approach where leaders intentionally identify, plan for, and integrate learning opportunities throughout the entire change process. It moves beyond simply executing a change plan to actively using the change as a catalyst for organizational and individual growth. That is, instead of just "doing" change, a learning agenda, according to leadership authors Jim Kouzes and Barry Posner, ensures leaders are also "learning from" the change, allowing them to adapt, refine, and ultimately be more effective in future transformations. It embodies the spirit of an adaptive, agile organization. Questions such as these will help answer the question "are we learning?"

> *How will we define "learning" for this change? What kind of insights are most valuable?*
>
> *What is our plan for acting on what we learn? How will insights translate into adjustments?*
>
> *What are we learning right now that is different from our initial assumptions?*
>
> *Based on the data/feedback we've gathered, what is working well, and what is not?*
>
> *What were the most significant lessons we learned from this change initiative?*[10]

- When considering a new initiative, you need more than just good intentions. Before making plans for a new effort, determine if additional learning is necessary for effective planning. Questions to consider are:

  > *What do we know?*
  >
  > *What do we not know?*
  >
  > *How can we learn what we still need to know?*

- Psychologist Gary Klein employs the concept of "premortem" to analyze a potential new endeavor. While "postmortems" begin after death, a "premortem" assumes the worst for the new undertaking. In this scenario, people are asked to imagine that it is a year from now, and the project has been a total fiasco. It failed miserably. Then they discuss the following question (and brainstorm proactive steps or contingency plans to prevent or mitigate the failure):

  > *Why did it fail?*[11]

- When presenting a proposal on behalf of a group that was asked to develop it, keep in mind that those hearing the report may be reluctant to ask tough questions for fear of appearing disrespectful of your hard work. One way to invite their active engagement could come from posing this question to them upon presenting the report:

   We doubt that our plan is the definitive answer, so we want to ask you,

   "What ideas come to mind for improving this plan?"

- With the advent of AI, it may be all too convenient to find "easy" answers. Having a learning agenda forces critical thinking about how to build on the content provided and provide depth and experience to any "results." In this regard, you have to ask:

   What else do I need to know and where can I search for that?

   What's worth fact-checking?

   How can I enrich the information provided and expand on it?

   What happens to the response when I reverse-engineer it or throw doubts on the conclusions?

Notes

1. Rosabeth M. Kanter, *The Change Masters: Innovation for Productivity in the American Corporation* (New York: Simon & Schuster, 1983).
2. Edgar H. Schein and Peter A. Schein, *Organizational Culture and Leadership* 5th ed. (San Francisco: Jossey-Bass, 2017).
3. Lisa Bodell, *Why Simple Wins* (Brookline, MA: Bibliomotion, 2017), 104.

4. Steve Blank and Bob Dorf, *The Startup Owner's Manual: The Step-By-Step Guide for Building a Great Company*, (Hoboken, NJ: John Wiley & Sons, 2020).
5. Elizabeth Lotardo, "Stop Solving Your Team's Problems for Them," *Harvard Business Review* (July 14, 2025), https://hbr.org/2025/07/stop-solving-your-teams-problems-for-them.
6. Woody Wade, *Scenario Planning: A Field Guide to the Future*. (Hoboken, NJ: John Wiley & Sons, 2012).
7. Paul J. H. Schoemaker, "Scenario Planning: A Tool for Strategic Thinking," *Sloan Management Review*, Vol. 36, No. 2 (1995), 25–40.
8. Terry J. Fadem, *The Art of Asking: Ask Better Questions, Get Better Answers* (Upper Saddle River, NJ: Financial Times Press, 2009), 115.
9. John P. Kotter, *Leading Change* (Boston: Harvard Business Review Press, 1996).
10. James M. Kouzes and Barry Z. Posner, *Learning Leadership: The Five Fundamentals of Becoming an Exemplary Leader* (Hoboken, NJ: John Wiley & Sons, 2016).
11. Gary Klein, "Performing a Project Premortem," *Harvard Business Review*, Vol. 85, No. 9 (2007), 18–19.

5
Innovation

Changes are always happening. Some are modest and incremental. However, leadership is required these days, given the rapid pace of social, environmental, economic, political, and technological developments. Leaders play a special role in developing a culture that supports and encourages innovation. The future will be built on such new ideas and breakthroughs. Consider the turnaround experience of the Danish company LEGO, building innovation from brick to brick.

In the late 1990s and early 2000s, The LEGO Group faced a severe crisis. The company had over-expanded into theme parks, video games, and clothing, introducing numerous unprofitable toy lines, such as Galidor—an action-figure series that departed from its core brick system and ultimately flopped, contributing to near bankruptcy by 2003.

1. **Leading Innovation:** In 2004, LEGO appointed Jørgen Vig Knudstorp—its first nonfamily CEO—to halt financial decline and restore liquidity. He quickly imposed tight fiscal controls, cutting 1,200 jobs, streamlining production, divesting noncore assets such as theme parks, and centralizing operations.
2. **Engaging Creativity:** Knudstorp emphasized disciplined innovation: LEGO slashed its inventory by half, focusing on building sets that aligned with its "system of play." It diversified

within its ecosystem through licensed lines such as Star Wars, Harry Potter, and Bionicle, thereby restoring market excitement. In parallel, LEGO embraced open innovation. It launched Cuusoo (later LEGO Ideas) in 2008—a platform where fans could propose designs, and if a concept received 10,000 votes (e.g., Minecraft), LEGO would consider turning it into an official set, sharing profits with creators.

3. **Assessing the Past and Present:** LEGO revisited its heritage, reaffirming the plastic brick system and the "stud-and-tube" interlock invented in the 1950s as the company's creative anchor. Simultaneously, it applied modern management practices, including the implementation of disciplined project oversight. For example, new product teams had to demonstrate minimum profit margins (~13.5%) before launching.

4. **Anticipating the Future:** Beyond brick sets, LEGO expanded thoughtfully, launching lines for adults like Architecture, and integrating technology with Life of George (2011), blending physical and digital play. It also fostered creativity and collaboration internally through LEGO Serious Play, a methodology that institutions have adopted globally for strategic thinking. Today, LEGO has adopted digital co-creation (e.g., Mindstorms and LEGO Ideas), ensuring that its next breakthroughs will be both internally engineered and crowd-validated.

By 2014, LEGO overtook Mattel as the world's largest toy company. Its journey exemplifies how visionary leadership, creative engagement, continuous assessment, and future-focused thinking can drive transformational innovation.

* * * * *

Leading Innovation

Questions

- Innovation is on the minds of all leaders as old ways of serving seem inadequate in today's not-business-as-usual context, and new models are sought. Having studied diverse settings where innovation had occurred, researchers concluded that the critical question for leaders is not "How do I make innovation happen?" but, instead:

How do I set the stage for innovation to happen?[1]

- Innovations can be exciting or threatening, depending on your perspective. Some people will be more excited and welcoming of the change than others. Apart from the specifics of the innovation, how you, as a leader, implement the change will either enhance the trust people have in you or diminish your credibility. Technology futurist Daniel Burrus suggests using this question in approaching any upcoming change:

Will the way I handle this innovation raise, maintain, or diminish trust?[2]

- While leadership is always about innovation, actually changing is not necessarily the first action for any leader. Jim Collins and Jerry Porras, in examining organizations that prospered and survived over time, assert that "contrary to popular wisdom, the proper first response to a changing world is not to ask, 'How should we change?'" They suggest the better first question is:

What do we stand for and why do we exist?

This should never change. And then, feel free to change everything else.[3]

- Ronald Heifetz, founding director of the Center for Public Leadership at Harvard University's Kennedy School, proposes that leaders begin tackling issues for which there is already a sense of urgency among people. He calls this urgency the "ripeness" of a challenge. The question he suggests for testing such ripeness is:

> ***Has the issue fastened in people's minds?***[4]

- Leaders tend to be good at suggesting changes. The challenge, however, lies in guiding people toward actual innovation. Management consultants Jeffrey and Laurie Ford suggest that in leading a new initiative, leaders should be clear about their *What-When-Why* message by using these questions:

    > ***What do we want to accomplish?***
    >
    > ***When do we want it to happen?***
    >
    > ***Why does it matter?***[5]

- Leaders often have opportunities to know what is happening within organizations similar to theirs. Because of that, a helpful question to ask is:

    > ***What innovations and initiatives do I see happening in organizations like ours that warrant consideration and discussion in my own organization?***

- When people have been in a leadership role for a while, it becomes difficult to see what's going on with fresh eyes. They can fall into the trap of working within the bounds of what they have done in the past to address challenges. Hal Gregersen, former director of the MIT Leadership Center, offers the following question as one way to realize a different perspective:

If someone new took over my position today, what would they probably do that we're not doing now?[6]

- Jim Kouzes and Barry Posner contend that when leaders are at their personal best, they "treat every job as an adventure." Stuff happens in organizations and people's lives, so it isn't critical whether you find the challenges or they find you. What is important, they maintain, is this: When opportunity knocks, are you prepared? Are you ready to open the door? Even if you've been in your job for years, treat today as if it were your first day, and ask yourself:

If I were just starting this job, what would I do? Begin doing those things now.

What are those projects that I've always wanted to undertake but never have?

Ask your team members to do the same.[7]

Encouraging Creativity

Questions

- Consider seeking clues for how to innovate through a process of "reversal." For example, a newly promoted division leader was eager to demonstrate growth within her division. She was able to develop a set of plans to expand the division's productivity simply by reversing the answers to an unusual question, which gave them a different angle, stimulating their creativity:

If we wanted our sales to decline in the next year, what are the things we might do to accomplish this goal?

- Some scholars contend that leaders spend far too much time with the wrong questions, such as only asking operational questions that begin with "how." Instead, these questions are more likely to challenge assumptions and conventional wisdom:

    > *Why?*
    >
    > *Why not?*
    >
    > *What if?*[8]

- Studies into how the brain processes information suggest that to see things differently and more creatively, you have to bombard your brain with things it has never encountered. Gregory Burns, director of Emory University's Center for Neuropolicy, explains that novelty is vital because the brain, which evolved for efficiency, routinely takes perceptual shortcuts to save energy. Forcing yourself to break free of habitual thinking patterns is how you get the brain to recategorize information. Consider how you might stir imagination by asking:

    > *How would Disney handle client relationships?*
    >
    > *How would FedEx address this logical problem?*
    >
    > *How would Korn Ferry go about recruiting?*
    >
    > *How would the FBI investigate this matter?*
    >
    > *How would our competitors respond to this change?*[9]

- When people are discussing something important to them, their knee-jerk thoughts tend to be about the arguments they want to advance in the debate. Often, a more powerful contribution you can make to the conversation is to pause and ask yourself in this situation:

    > *What are the questions I should be asking?*

- When discussions of big problems appear most overwhelming and solutions are not coming, questions for brainstorming might be:

  If we had all the money in the world, how would we solve this problem?

  If we had all the time in the world, how would we solve this problem?

  Assuming we do not have all the time or money in the world, how can we scale down these solutions to work within our limitations?[10]

- You may have heard a variation of this saying by the French essayist Emile Chartier: "Nothing is more dangerous than an idea when it is the only one you have." Developing options can stimulate creativity in ways that stopping with one answer does not. A good question to use when a group is about to settle on a plan is:

  That is undoubtedly one good solution. What might another solution be?

- Peter Senge, founder of the Society for Organizational Learning, says that good news travels upward in an organization faster than the speed of light, but failure is ignored or denied. To assess openness to innovation for any organization, he suggests asking:

  How fast does bad news travel upward?[11]

Assessing the Past and Present

Questions

- While seemingly counterintuitive, you must first look back into the past when aiming for the future. Looking backward permits you to see further into the future because it enables you to identify themes, patterns, and beliefs that underscore both what you care about and why before moving forward. According to John Seaman and George David Smith, a company's history can be a leadership tool. Spend some time reflecting on the question:

How did I (we) get to where I am (we are) today?

How did we arrive at our current state?[12]

- Michael Watkins, noted scholar on accelerating transitions, says that without a historical perspective, you run the risk of tearing down fences without knowing why they were put up in the first place. Armed with historical insight, you may determine that the wall is no longer needed and can be removed. Alternatively, you may find there is a good reason to leave it where it is. Consider asking:

Why do we do the things we are now doing?

Why were the current policies, practices, and processes put into place?[13]

- The future is always uncertain. The future is the domain of leaders, as no one can guarantee what tomorrow holds for us or our organizations. Some valuable perspectives for thinking about the future, rather than simply worrying about it, according to technology futurist Daniel Burrus, arise from asking:

In a world filled with uncertainty, what are you sure about?

What problems are you about to have, and how can you solve them before they happen?

What actions should you take now to have a better future?[14]

- When Lars Sørensen was named the number-one business CEO by the *Harvard Business Review*, he was asked what other companies might learn from his innovation strategies. As head of a Danish company founded in the 1920s that provides most of the insulin used in the world today, he suggested three questions that needed to be asked:

   What are our strengths?

   What are our capabilities?

   What risks do we dare take?[15]

- One question that shifts groups from the common tendency to focus on things that are not working, or needing to be fixed, is to switch or revise the thinking and perspective by asking:

   What's working, and how can we do more of it?

- Start paying more attention to what's going on around you right now. The directions and turns the world will take are embedded in the past and the present. You often recognize them retrospectively, but the clues are all around you right now. Where are they hiding? Ask yourself:

   What are people doing now that they weren't doing a few years ago?

   What are today's hot topics? What are people talking about now that they weren't in the past?

   What are people no longer paying attention to?

   What are people complaining about these days that is different?

   What am I hearing about or paying attention to these days that is new?

- In *Leading the Revolution*, Gary Hamel, one of the world's most influential business thinkers, observed that many people don't appreciate and comprehend what's changing around them "because they're down at ground level, lost in the thicket of confusing, conflicting data." He maintains that you have to make time to step back and ask yourself:

   What's the big story that cuts across all these little facts?[16]

Anticipating the Future

Questions

- A handy way for leaders to focus on the long-term frame of reference for their groups and organizations is to ask:

   What is happening today that will change the world in the next 5 to 10 years?

- Leaders are quite literally their organization's "futures department." "What's next?" should be the question you are frequently asking. One powerful way to prospect the future is to consider this question:

   What question or questions, if answered, could make the most difference to the future of our organization?[17]

- Leaders find themselves feeling too often like "crisis managers" because, as futurist Daniel Burrus writes in *Flash Foresight*, they devote too little time, regularly, to becoming an "anticipatory leader" for an "anticipatory organization" that solves problems before they become a crisis. To do this, he suggests that leaders and groups look into the visible future and ask:

What are the problems I'm about to have?[18]

- Surveying the landscape in which your organization operates is always significant and should be an ongoing process. The future is where opportunity lies. These four questions will help:

    What are three trends affecting us today?

    Which will make the most impact?

    How should we prepare?

    What steps can we take?

- As Wharton scholar and researcher Adam Grant explains, "Predicting the future is hard. No one is right most of the time. But it's possible to be wrong less often." Grant, in reviewing data from a forecasting tournament, observed that those who were more accurate at forecasting had the mindset of a scientist, in contrast to those of what he called a preacher, prosecutor, or politician. They treated their predictions as hypotheses to be tested, rather than hard facts to be confirmed, and tended to be humbler about what they knew. They were open to challenging their own convictions and curious about seeking out other ideas and people who might contradict their thoughts. When thinking ahead, he says you need to think again:

    What are my assumptions, and do they still make sense?

    Am I sufficiently humble to admit what I don't know and open to learning new things?[19]

- Envisioning the future is much like composers finding a musical theme from all the notes that swirl about in their heads. Reflect on the fundamental values and beliefs that consistently recur in your life. Consider the causes you contribute to in various ways and those to which you don't pay attention. To gain some insights about the future, Santa Clara University Professors Don Polden and Barry Posner suggest you ask yourself:

  What are the issues that keep popping up on my radar?

  What things keep me up at night or get me jumping out of bed in the morning?

  What are the "I wish . . ." statements that you find yourself echoing?[20]

Notes

1. Linda A. Hill, Greg Brandeau, Emily Truelove, and Kent Lineback, "Collective Genius," *Harvard Business Review*, Vol. 92, Issue 6 (June 2014).
2. Daniel Burrus, *Flash Foresight: How to See the Invisible and Do the Impossible* (New York: HarperCollins, 2011), 244.
3. Jim Collins and Jerry I. Porras, *Built to Last: Successful Habits of Visionary Companies* (New York: HarperCollins, 2011), xiv.
4. Ronald Heifetz, *Leadership Without Easy Answers* (Cambridge, MA: Belknap Press, 1994), 116.
5. Jeffrey Ford and Laurie Ford, *The Four Conversations: Daily Communication That Gets Results* (Oakland, CA: Berrett-Koehler Publishers, 2009), 41.
6. Hal Gregersen, "Bursting the CEO Bubble: Why Executives Should Talk Less and Ask More Questions," *Harvard Business Review*, Vol. 95, No. 2 (March–April 2017), 81–89.
7. James M. Kouzes and Barry Z. Posner, *The Leadership Challenge: How to Make Extraordinary Things Happen in Organizations*, 7th Ed. (Hoboken, NJ: John Wiley & Sons, 2023), 161.

8. Jeffrey H. Dyer, Hal B. Gregersen, and Clayton M. Christensen, "The Innovator's DNA," *Harvard Business Review*, Vol. 87, Issue 12 (December 2009), 63.
9. Gregory Burns, *Iconoclast: A Neuroscientist Reveals How to Think Differently* (Boston: Harvard Business School Press, 2008).
10. Dorothy Leeds, *The Seven Powers of Questions* (New York: Perigee, 2000), 59–60.
11. Peter M. Senge, "The Practice of Innovation," *Leader to Leader*, Vol. 9 (Summer 1998), 21–27.
12. John T. Seaman Jr and George D. Smith, "Your Company's History as a Leadership Tool," *Harvard Business Review*, Vol. 90, Issue 12 (December 2012), 146–154
13. Michel D. Watkins, *The First 90 Days: Proven Strategies for Getting Up to Speed Faster and Smarter, Updated and Expanded* (Boston: Harvard Business Review Press, 2013).
14. Daniel Burrus, *op. cit.*, 247.
15. Adi Ignatius and Daniel McGinn, "Novo Nordisk CEO Lars Sørensen on What Propelled Him to the Top," *Harvard Business Review*, Vol. 93, Issue 11 (November 2015), 65.
16. Gary Hamel, *Leading the Revolution* (Boston: Harvard Business School Press, 2000), 128.
17. Eric E. Vogt, Juanita Brown, and David Isaacs, *The Art of Powerful Questions: Catalyzing Insight, Innovation, and Action* (Mill Valley, CA: Whole Systems Associates, 2003), 12.
18. Daniel Burrus, *op. cit.*, 45.
19. Adam Grant, *Think Again: The Power of Knowing What You Don't Know* (New York: Viking, 2021), 55–76.
20. Donald J. Polden and Barry Z. Posner, *Lawyers as Leaders: Why It Matters and What It Takes* (Chicago: American Bar Association, 2024), 42.

6 | Making Good Decisions

Making decisions is an integral part of a leader's job. However, leadership decisions, unlike many personal choices, must consider far more than one's individual preference. Leaders always serve within a context and are stewards of a larger mission, both of which have claims on the decisions they must make. Decisions move change forward because every decision means changes, and again, change is the province of leadership.

Regardless of the setting and situation, decision-making is complex because typically one decision leads to another decision, and so on. For leaders, there is no dearth of decision-making opportunities. There is an expression that "one bad decision leads to another," and, unfortunately, this can be true. Much like the experience of a sailor or engineer, a small error at the beginning of a voyage or a small mistake in the design of software will have enormous consequences farther down the line. Accordingly, for carpenters, the ironclad mantra is "measure twice, cut once."

Leaders develop and hone their capacity to make effective decisions over time, particularly shaped by their on-the-job experiences. Good decisions are reflections of good judgment, and leaders make judgment calls all the time. Where to spend time, money, and resources in general, whether or not to open a new business or partner with a controversial client, expand locations or services, who to hire, how to incentivize and promote . . . the list goes on as examples of the decisions commonly made by leaders that are strongly shaped based on their judgment.

How is good judgment acquired? The straightforward answer is that it is gained through experience. Illustrating the point, presidential advisor and lawyer Ted Sorenson recounted this story about how lawyers acquire judgment:

> *A new associate happens to be seated at lunch next to a senior partner, and the younger person says to the veteran, "Tell me, why is it you have this big reputation for judgment?"*
>
> *"Well," the partner replies, "there are people who seem to respect my judgment."*
>
> *"If you don't mind my asking another question, why do they respect your judgment?"*
>
> *"Well, I guess I've made the right decision enough times," the partner says.*
>
> *"If you don't mind me bothering you, what was the basis on which you made the right decision?"*
>
> *"Oh," the partner replies, "that comes from experience."*
>
> *"One last question: What's the experience based on?"*
>
> *"Wrong decisions," the partner replies.*[1]

As you hone your decision-making abilities and judgment, consider the questions you should ask to get started, ensuring that you test your assumptions, explore options, and assess the impact before you decide.

Getting Started

Questions

- Decision-making is not easy. Questions such as these serve as a starting point for approaching what appears to be a complex situation:

  What is the primary goal of the decision?

  What information do we need to make a decision?

  How will we get this information?

- Deciding among competing priorities with limited time, energy, and resources is always a challenge. Before making any decision, ask yourself:

  Even if we achieve the results we are seeking, will it justify the time, effort, and money we will have to invest in this initiative?

- So much effort goes into trying to fix problems that leaders sometimes fail to ask more basic questions, such as:

  Why do we have this problem in the first place?

  What will happen if we decide to not make a decision?

- All of us have a bias toward the familiar. Best-selling authors and academics Chip Heath and Dan Heath suggest questions that can mitigate against doing only what first comes to mind:

  How can you expand your options?

  How can you get outside your head and collect information that you can trust?

> *How can you overcome short-term emotions and conflicted feelings to make the best choice?*
>
> *How can you plan for an uncertain future in a way that gives your decisions the best chance to succeed?*[2]

- When faced with decisions, leaders and groups often consider too narrow a range of options. One way to expand alternatives is rather than beginning with the question, "What should we do?" begin with the prior question about:

  > *What could we do?*[3]

- Listening to people with diverse viewpoints helps you avoid blind spots. Challenge your thinking by asking:

  > *Who disagrees with me, and why?*
  >
  > *What are some of the best counterarguments?*
  >
  > *What am I not considering, or accounting for, or ignoring, or missing?*

Testing Assumptions

Questions

- All leaders bring unspoken assumptions to any planning or decision-making process. Therefore, it can be helpful to ask yourself:

  > *What assumptions underlie my thinking, and are they valid?*
  >
  > *What if my assumptions are wrong—how would that change the options?*

Am I addressing the right problem, or just the obvious one?

Am I choosing this option because it's safe, familiar, or is it truly the best?

- The Japanese organizational theorist and management consultant Kenichi Ohmae maintains that a good strategist makes a habit of challenging prevailing assumptions by relentlessly asking the same question about the current way of doing things. That simple question is:

   Why?[4]

- When plans for a new endeavor are taking shape, those closest to the planning process should be asking questions such as:

   What are the assumptions embedded in the plans?

   Which of these assumptions must prove true for this project to succeed?

   What is the likelihood that the assumptions are correct?

   Do we need to test these assumptions before proceeding?[5]

- Peter Bregman is the CEO of a company that helps senior leaders create accountability and inspire collective action on their organization's most important work. He describes a two-question sequence that works superbly when introducing a new idea, procedure, or plan.

About halfway through your presentation, introduce the first question:

Why won't this work for you?

Whatever feedback or comments you receive, your response is the same: "That's a good point," followed by this second question:

So, how can you change it to make it work?[6]

- It is not an all-too-uncommon trap to get stuck in the "way things have always been done," letting routine overshadow innovation. To break free and spark new ideas, ask questions that challenge assumptions and push the boundaries of current thinking:

    Why do we do it this way? What if we stopped doing this entirely?

    Who else has solved a similar problem, and what can we learn from them?

    If our product or service didn't exist, what would our users or customers do instead?

    What would our competitor do if they wanted to put us out of business?

    What could we create today that would be considered impossible five years ago?

Exploring Options

Questions

- Sometimes an idea will be suggested in a meeting about which there is some interest but also skepticism about whether it will work. A question for that situation might be:

    Suppose we did it that way . . . what would happen?

- Researchers have found that "whether or not" decisions (that is, deciding between only two options) fail 52% of the time. In contrast, decisions made after considering more than two options failed only 32% of the time. "Whether or not" decisions cause leaders to ask the wrong questions, such as "How can I make this work?" or "How can I get my colleagues behind me?" A more effective way to proceed is to ask:

   Is there a better way?

   What else could we do?[7]

- Joseph L. Badaracco teaches business ethics at Harvard Business School and has written extensively about the importance of character in leadership. He suggests these five practical questions to help improve decision-making when information is incomplete, and opinions are divided.

   What are the net, net consequences of all my options?

   What are my core obligations?

   What will work in the world as it is?

   Who are we?

   What can I live with?[8]

- The "Vanishing Options Test" is a way to help leaders and groups expand their options for action. The heart of the exercise comes from this question:

   If we cannot choose any of the current options being considered, what else could we do?[9]

- Stanford Professor Debra Meyerson suggests several questions to ask when fearing the consequences of potential actions:

  > *What might happen if you take this course of action?*
  >
  > *What are the worst things that could happen?*
  >
  > *Why are you so afraid of these outcomes?*
  >
  > *How bad would it be if feared outcomes materialize?*[10]

- Sometimes, fears about the decision not being accepted or not working out well may lead leaders to hold back from trying new or novel ideas. If you have ideas you are reluctant to advance, ask yourself this question:

  > *What's a safe way for me to test out the wisdom of an idea I've had for some time but never acted upon?*

- It is often helpful to ask this question or a variation of it before moving forward on a project or decision to make sure nothing has been missed.

  > *Have we overlooked any information or perspectives that we should take into consideration?*

- When there appear to be continuing reservations by one or more people to a decision a group is planning to make, these questions may help uncover those concerns and provide additional options:

  > *What are your major apprehensions about this action?*
  >
  > *What other options do you see to accomplish the same goal?*

- The single most effective question that Chip Heath and Dan Heath say they have found for helping to break a decision logjam is:

  What would I tell my best friend to do in this situation?[11]

- Good leaders build up credibility over time. Joseph Badaracco, Jr., suggests three questions to use when considering an effort that may risk using up some of that goodwill:

  How much organizational capital do I have?

  How much am I placing at risk?

  What are the likely rewards for others and yourself?[12]

Assessing the Impact

Questions

- There is a temptation to make decisions that seem right in the moment but may not be the best for the future. *New York Times* bestselling author, business journalist, and television commentator Suzy Welch has a method to help put immediate feelings into a longer-frame perspective. It is called 10/10/10 and utilizes three questions to ask about decisions:

  How will we feel about it in 10 minutes?

  How about 10 months from now?

  How about 10 years from now?[13]

- Scholar and best-selling author Jim Collins says that great enterprises take risks while avoiding ones that might jeopardize their future. When there is uncertainty about possible new and chancy ventures, he suggests three questions:

    What's the upside if events turn out well?

    What's the downside if events go very badly?

    Can I live with the downside?[14]

- Tim Cook, CEO of Apple, has said that too often, company leaders ask the wrong question when it comes to issues that impact others and the public at large. The question, he contends, should not be "How much can we get away with?" but rather:

    "What are the consequences?"[15]

- It is tempting to think that when a plan is finalized, the challenging work is over. Instead, it is just beginning. Before sharing new possibilities, be sure to ask these questions:

    Do I understand the questions, interests, and concerns of critical stakeholders?

    How should I tailor my message to suit different groups based on their interests?

- According to two of Santa Clara University's former deans Don Polden (Law) and Barry Posner (Business), an often overlooked or neglected aspect of decision making is gauging the decisions' validity and effectiveness against the actual course of events. They suggest taking some time to reflect on the entire process and consider what was done that is worth repeating, as well as what you realize you would do differently in the future. Ask yourself:

Did the decision make a difference?[16]

Notes

1. As quoted in Noel M. Tichy and Warren G. Bennis, *Judgment: How Winning Leaders Make Great Calls* (New York: Portfolio, 2007), 9–10.
2. Chip Heath and Dan Heath, *Decisive: How to Make Better Choices in Life and Work* (New York: Crown Business, 2013), 23.
3. John Beshears and Francesca Gino, "Leaders as Decision Architects," *Harvard Business Review*, Vol. 93, Issue 5 (May/June 2015), 59.
4. Kenichi Ohmae, *The Mind of the Strategist: The Art of Japanese Business* (New York: McGraw-Hill, 1982).
5. Clayton M. Christensen, James Allworth, and Karen Dillon, *How Will You Measure Your Life?* (New York: HarperCollins, 2012), 56–57.
6. Peter Bregman, *18 Minutes: Find Your Focus, Master Distraction, and Get the Right Things Done* (New York: Business Plus, 2011), 234.
7. Chip Heath and Dan Heath, *op. cit.*, 37.
8. Joseph L. Badaracco, "How to Tackle Your Toughest Decisions," *Harvard Business Review*, Vol. 94, Issue 9 (September 2016), 104–107.
9. Chip Heath and Dan Heath, *op. cit.*, 46.
10. Debra E. Meyerson, *Rocking the Boat: How to Effect Change without Making Trouble* (Boston: Harvard Business Press, 2008), 92.
11. Chip Heath and Dan Heath, *op. cit.*, 172.
12. Joseph L. Badaracco Jr, *Leading Quietly* (Boston: Harvard Business School Press, 2002), 78.
13. Suzy Welch, *10-10-10: A Life-Transitioning Idea* (New York: Scribner, 2009).

14. Jim Collins, *How the Mighty Fall: And Why Some Companies Never Give In* (New York: HarperCollins, 2009), 74.
15. Justin Bariso, "Tim Cook May Have Just Ended Facebook," *Inc.com* (January 30, 2021), https://www.inc.com/justin-bariso/tim-cook-may-have-just-ended-facebook.html.
16. Donald J. Polden and Barry Z. Posner, *Lawyers as Leaders: Why It Matters and What It Takes* (Chicago: American Bar Association, 2024), 117.

7

Personnel Matters

As we indicated in the previous chapter, leaders make decisions. One of the most important involves hiring, which many call the most critical decision a leader makes to "get the right people on the bus." Leaders live and die by the quality and continuity of those who, as Jim Kouzes and Barry Posner put it, "want to struggle for shared aspirations."[1] The selection, development, and support of quality people sets a tone for the entire organization. Leadership requires mobilizing others; it is a team effort, and few decisions are more critical than those involving personnel.

However, your responsibility as a leader doesn't stop with opening the front door to new hires or getting them situated at their desk or workplace. Leadership is not a solo act; nothing great was ever accomplished as the result of a single person's efforts. It takes a village; it's a team effort, and you have a responsibility not only to be great yourself but also to create the conditions where others can lead, act, and contribute meaningfully.

A key ingredient in Alan Mulally's turnaround of the Ford Motor Company involved inviting others to lead, rather than centralizing control or micromanaging.[2] He delegated authority, broke down silos, and encouraged open communication across departments. He emphasized collaboration and mutual support. He trained and mentored his executive team, coached leaders to speak openly, take ownership, and lead their own teams with the same approach. Mulally didn't save Ford alone; he built a system that allowed others to lead.

Wendy Kopp founded Teach For America (TFA) with a bold vision: to end educational inequity by recruiting high-potential college graduates to teach in underserved schools.[3] The idea wasn't just to place teachers—it was to develop future leaders committed to systemic change in education. TFA focused heavily on mentorship, training, and leadership development. Corps members were provided with support networks, coaches, and tools to help them lead effectively in challenging environments. Alumni were encouraged to start new organizations, run for school boards, and lead schools and nonprofits. Thousands of TFA alumni hold leadership roles, including superintendents, policymakers, school boards, and founders of nonprofit organizations.

For Mulally and Kopp, their leadership legacy was not just about turning around Ford or increasing the quality of students' education; it was also about transforming followers into leaders. The best leaders know that they "can't do it alone." Asking the right questions will help you find the best people for your organization and also ensure that they grow and develop.

★ ★ ★ ★ ★

When There's an Opening

Questions

- When a staff position opens, you should avoid the trap of recruiting and hiring a new person under the same terms as the previous staff person. In most cases, it is valuable to ask questions such as:

> *What are the implications for this position in light of other competing needs we have?*

> *Would it make sense to leave this position open for a few months to see if it is still needed or needed in the same configuration?*

- Whenever someone leaves your employment, it is a good opportunity to reassess the position and its purposes. Possible questions may be:

   > *What are all the staff needs we currently have, including those covered by this position?*

   > *Which ones are most essential to cover at this time?*

   > *How might we use this opening, plus other restructuring or redefining of positions, to address as many needs as we can?*

- Frances Hesselbein, as president of the Girl Scouts of the USA, sought to create an organization in which "every girl could see herself." Each hiring opportunity offers the chance to reflect on questions, Hesselbein said, that were necessary to implement that aspiration. Consider your own team or organization's mission:

   > *Do our leaders see themselves as the embodiment of the mission, values, and beliefs of the organization?*

   > *Are we deploying leaders, teams, and people to further the mission and achieve our goals?*

   > *Are we leading from the front, anticipating change rather than reacting to it?*

   > *Are we building today the richly diverse, inclusive, cohesive organization that our vision and mission demand?*[4]

- Fairness and inclusion remain crucial in cultivating a world-class workforce. Questions that may help you realize the benefit from doing so include:

  Do I seek out people with views different from my own?

  Do I associate with and learn from people different from me?

  Am I able to draw from ideas that come from beyond my interests and expertise?

  Can I make connections among all the information and experiences available to me?

- To ensure candidates can be effectively interviewed and assessed, you and others on the recruiting and hiring team need to clarify:

  What are the three to five core competencies this position requires?

Interviewing

Questions

- Job interview questions can often provide little useful information because the questions and answers are so predictable. Consider asking questions that require the candidate to reveal more about themselves, such as:

  What did you learn in your first job (or most recent job)?

  Tell us about a work success you have had, what happened, and what you learned from it.

  Tell us about a problem you faced and how you solved it.

  Tell us about a work failure you have had, what happened, and what you learned from it.

- Warren Bennis, university president and leadership scholar, said that if he could ask someone being considered for a position only one question, it would be:

   Tell me about a mistake you made and how you dealt with it.[5]

- Jodi Goldstein, managing director of the Harvard Innovation Labs, says that when she was looking to hire new people, she looked for "amazing." She later learned that the ability to handle adversity was a more important trait, and here's the question she uses in interviewing:

   What's something that went wrong, and how did you deal with it?[6]

- Leaders grow by learning. Weak leaders struggle to recall their mistakes, while effective leaders can readily recount past failures and what they have learned. The key to learning from both successes and missteps is to ask both questions multiple times to see how well candidates remember their failures (and successes) and especially what they learned from them:

   Tell me about a time when you experienced a setback or failure.

   What did you learn from that experience?

   Tell me about a time when you achieved a successful outcome or accomplishment.

   What did you learn from that experience?

- Several intriguing questions that go beyond those promulgated in many self-help books, such as: "What would you do if you knew you could not fail?" according to journalist and author Elizabeth Gilbert, are:

    What would you do even if you knew that you might very well fail?

    What do you love doing so much that the words failure and success essentially become irrelevant?[7]

- If you are looking for someone with potential for innovation and creativity, look for wide-ranging interests, says David Epstein in his writing about "why generalists triumph in a specialized world." As the person describes their past work, keep in mind this question:

    Do they tend to focus on intersections with other systems and the work of others?[8]

- Keep the focus in your interviews on competencies required for the role, not on background, personality, or fit with a narrow "culture" by asking questions such as:

    Can you walk us through a recent project that demonstrates your ability to [key skill] (e.g., problem-solving, collaboration, leadership)?

    Can you describe a time you had to learn something new quickly to complete a task.

    Describe a situation where you had to work with someone very different from you. What was challenging, and what did you learn?

If you were asked to improve [a common situation in the role], how would you approach it?

Here's a hypothetical challenge—what steps would you take to address it?

Assessing Candidates

Questions

- Peter Drucker knew that perhaps the most important decisions leaders make involve the selection of people. He said that when multiple candidates are being considered for a position, the question should not be "What can this or that candidate do or not do?" It is better, he suggested, to ask the question:

    What are the strengths each candidate possesses, and are these the right strengths for this assignment?[9]

- Presumably, you have clearly defined the role and responsibilities of the position. The following questions, consequently, will help you in assessing candidates' qualifications and fit:

    Did this person demonstrate evidence of those competencies during the interview?

    How well did their experience align with the actual needs of this role?

    Did their responses show a capacity to grow into future challenges, not just current ones?

    Can this person do the job well based on what they've done and how they think?

> *Did they provide clear, specific examples of relevant achievements or problem-solving?*
>
> *How did they approach situational or task-based questions—did their thought process show sound judgment, creativity, or discipline?*
>
> *How did the candidate describe working with others, especially in conflict, disagreement, or diversity?*
>
> *Did they show a willingness to learn from mistakes or feedback?*
>
> *How have they grown or evolved in past roles?*
>
> *Can this person scale with the role as it evolves or expands?*

- Résumés and interviews are of limited value in hiring decisions compared to talking with people who know the candidate and are willing to speak with you about them. Questions for such "informants" might be:

    > *What were specific things this person accomplished?*
    >
    > *How would co-workers describe working with this person?*

- A common question to ask a previous employer is whether they would hire this person again. Renowned industrial psychologist and leading expert on hiring high-performers, Bradford Smart, suggests that if the answer is positive, consider following up with this question:

    > *In what capacity would you want to place this person the next time around?*[10]

- As you are evaluating applicants or candidates for promotion, take a few moments to get in touch with some of your potential biases. Harvard Business and Government Professor Iris Bohnet, offers these sample questions:

> *Am I favoring this candidate because they remind me of myself or someone I like?*
>
> *Would I feel differently about this answer if it came from a different demographic group?*
>
> *Have I challenged my assumptions about what success looks like in this role?*[11]

Removing Barriers

Questions

- A strong, engaged, and collaborative cadre of leaders is essential for ongoing organizational vitality. One of a leader's most important tasks is to identify and support new, emerging leaders. At the same time, even the most dedicated and dependable existing leaders need care and encouragement. All leaders throughout a system should see themselves as "leaders of leaders" in their sphere of responsibility, asking:

> *What barriers can I remove?*
>
> *In what ways can I engage people?*
>
> *How can I best develop and appreciate people?*

- It's not all that difficult to get started in removing barriers so that people can do what they do even better. At an upcoming meeting, ask participants to identify ways that they can better help one another:

  > *What do we do that gets in the way of your doing your work well?*

  > *What would be one rule, process, or policy that, if removed, would make us even more effective?*

- In *New Amsterdam*, Dr. Max Goodwin, the TV show's charismatic medical director, has a simple yet transformative catchphrase. It's a question he asks often, always genuinely intending to listen, act, and make a difference. This question reflects a mindset of service, empathy, and proactive problem-solving:

  > *How can I help?*

- Sometimes leaders neglect to make sure staff and volunteers have what they need to do their jobs well. Pose this question to the people you work and interact with, identifying feasible ways you can make others even more effective:

  > *Is there something you need right now that would help you perform your job more effectively?*

- Consider the possibility that you may be the barrier or roadblock that is keeping others from being at their best. Have the courage and humility to ask the people you work with such questions as these:

  > *Is there information (experience or perspective) that I have that would help you do your work better?*

> *What do I do that hampers or possibly blocks you?*
>
> *What, if anything, could I stop doing that would make your job/life more productive?*
>
> *What should I keep doing that helps you perform well?*
>
> *If it were in my power, what would you have me do that I'm now not doing?*

- If you have responsibility for overseeing the work of others, then you probably interact with them regularly. Some of these times are for planning, while others are for reviewing progress. Some conversations may be part of a formal annual or quarterly review process. A poignant question appropriate for any of these times, suggests Michael Lukaszewski, president and co-founder of Hopeware, is:

  > *Where do you need me more, and where do you need me less?*[12]

- Decades of research have shown that helping at work, though valuable, is all too rare. One way to improve the quality of help is to first push for clarity. Another approach is to avoid the politeness trap by making a direct and specific request. Finally, be sure that you close the loop. You can make use of questions like:

  > *What's blocking your progress?*
  >
  > *What outcome are you aiming for?*
  >
  > *What would you like me to do to help?*
  >
  > *Did you find my assistance helpful?*
  >
  > *What else could I have done to help?*[13]

Engaging

Questions

- Quint Studer, 2025 recipient of the Baldrige Foundation Leadership Excellence Award, makes it a point to ask several questions after someone's first few weeks on the job:

  > *How do we compare to what we said we would be like?*
  >
  > *Are there any lessons we can learn from your previous workplace?*
  >
  > *What is going well?*
  >
  > *Is there anything that might cause you to want to leave?*[14]

- When a new team is being formed to address a critical issue, you can help the proposed leader make sure to get the right people on the team (of course, the same applies if you are to be the new leader yourself). Consider posing such questions as:

  > *Is the team the right size to complete the task efficiently?*
  >
  > *Does the team comprise individuals with the necessary skills, expertise, and influence?*
  >
  > *How should members be selected (e.g., by appointment, election, representation, tenure, etc.)?*
  >
  > *Does the team capitalize on the organization's diversity?*[15]

- Helping people identify their values and finding ways those values can be lived out within their daily lives is essential to their growth and fulfillment. Consider engaging people in conversation with questions like:

What are your most cherished values?

How do you live them out in this organization?

What, if anything, can be done better to align your actions and decisions with your values?

- When you find yourself amid an effort in which everyone seems frustrated by a lack of progress, it may help to regroup with questions such as:

  Where are we now?

  Where do we need to be?

  What do we need to do to get there?

- The venture capitalist John Doerr suggests several questions to help people to both take stock of where they are now and to get them to think about the future:

  What are you working on?

  How are you doing?

  Is there anything impeding your work?

  What do you need to be more successful?

  How do you need to grow to achieve your goals?[16]

- Performance reviews tend to be crowded out by other things, especially those that come outside of any required annual assessments. Increasingly, organizations are finding that incorporating "along the way" conversations, ideally held quarterly, benefits everyone. For example, ask:

What recent success has meant much to you?

What is your most important goal in the coming months?

What do you need to achieve that goal?

- Performance evaluation sessions are not usually anyone's favorite conversations. Of course, they are much easier when everything has been going well. Even still, the session would benefit all parties when a few probing questions such as these are included:

What would make you want to stay here longer?

Can you envision something happening here that would make you consider leaving?

What external factors might lure you away?

- Former Army Intelligence officer Neil Petrie says that one question you can ask to gauge the extent to which people are taking ownership for their growth and development as leaders is:

What is the one thing you are working on that will require you to grow to accomplish it?[17]

- Marshall Goldsmith, in his role as an executive coach, begins by meeting with the people with whom the leader regularly interacts. These are some of the questions he asks them about that leader:

Does this person communicate a vision?

Do they treat people with respect?

Do they solicit contrary opinions?

Do they encourage other people's ideas?

Do they listen to other people in meetings?[18]

Handling Differences

Questions

- There is no need to fear differences. The goal is not to abolish differences, as if we could, but rather to find ways to engage our differences in ways that can affirm all people and their perspectives while still making progress toward common goals. When someone makes statements that do not seem to match your perceptions, questions from which to draw are:

  On what information do you base your comments?

  What experience convinced you of this?

- When you find yourself in the midst of conflict, your objectivity might be hard to maintain. A question to help do a reality check might be to ask yourself:

  What do the most objective people who are aware of the dynamics of the situation think about what has happened and what should happen next?

- Sometimes your questions can be used to find common ground and move the discussion forward. For example:

  What aspects of my perspective resonate with you, even if you don't entirely agree?

  What do you think is the most significant difference between our views on this?

  If we were to find a solution that considers both our viewpoints, what might that look like?

  What are the non-negotiables for you in this situation, and what areas might be open for compromise?

  Is there any common ground we can identify that we both agree on, even if it's a minor point?

- New possibilities and perspectives can be explored when you ask questions such as these:

  What assumptions might we be making that are influencing our views?

  What are the potential benefits of considering an alternative approach (even if it's not your initial preference)?

  What might be some of the potential implications or outcomes of that?

  How can we ensure that differing concerns are addressed in any decision we make?

  What would need to happen for everyone involved to feel comfortable with [alternative idea/solution]?

- When differences, disagreements, and even conflicts are evident, you should have in mind some questions you can ask that elicit more information—without appearing or seeming to be adversarial. Help yourself and other conflicting parties to better understanding by asking questions like:

> *Could you tell me more about what leads you to that conclusion?*
>
> *Can you help me understand the specific points that are most important to you here?*
>
> *Are there any specific details or examples that would help me grasp your point more fully?*

- Leaders have values and goals they want achieved. At the same time, they want to encourage others to contribute their perspectives and wisdom. Denise Brosseau, the founder and CEO of Thought Leadership Lab, suggests a question to keep in mind when presenting an idea:

    > *How can you best frame your ideas so that they remain strong and clear while allowing others with different views to hear and understand?*[19]

- Inexperienced leaders are often tempted to support new ideas they like and resist those that do not appeal to them. As leaders develop, they come to see that their task is not to decide "which side to join" but instead to help themselves and others think clearly about various options. Support or opposition makes no sense until differing options are reviewed with probing questions. Consider asking:

    > *Can you tell me more about why this idea makes sense?*
    >
    > *Why do you think we haven't done something like this before?*

What would have to change if we implemented this idea?

Who have you consulted with already about this idea? What do they say?

- Meetings and committee sessions are often filled with people offering many different opinions on the topic under consideration. Some contributions are likely to be more informed than others. But frequently, for the sake of harmony, ideas are not sufficiently questioned. Doing so requires adopting a tone that is inviting and communicates that you are genuinely seeking added information and perspectives. Possible questions to pose at such times are:

What leads you to say that?

That is an interesting idea. Can you give an example?

What experiences or information have shaped your perspective on this?

Is there particular evidence that leads you to that conclusion?

Notes

1. James M. Kouzes and Barry Z. Posner, *The Leadership Challenge: How to Make Extraordinary Things Happen in Organizations*, 7th ed (Hoboken, NJ: John Wiley & Sons, 2023), 18.
2. Bryce G. Hoffman, *American Icon: Alan Mulally and the Fight to Save Ford Motor Company* (New York: Crown Currency, 2015).
3. Wendy Kopp, *A Chance to Make History: What Works and What Doesn't in Providing an Excellent Education for All* (New York: Public Affairs, 2012).
4. Francis Hesselbein, "Community Partners Who Inspire," *Leader to Leader*, Vol. 96 (Spring 2000), 4–6.
5. Warren Bennis and Robert Townsend, *Reinventing Leadership*. Audio tape, Simon and Schuster, 1996.
6. Adam Bryant, "Humility is the Mother of Invention: An Interview with Jodi Goldstein," *New York Times*, November 20, 2016.

7. Elizabeth Gilbert, *Big Magic: Creative Living Beyond Fear* (New York: Riverhead Books, 2015), 259.
8. David Epstein, *Range: Why Generalists Triumph in a Specialized World* (New York: Riverhead Books, 2019), 213.
9. Peter Drucker, "The Peter F. Drucker Reader: Selected Articles from the Father of Modern Management Thinking," (Harvard Business Review Press, 2016).
10. Bradford D. Smart, *Topgrading: How Leading Companies Win by Hiring, Coaching, and Keeping the Best People* (New York: Portfolio, 2005).
11. Iris Bohnet, *What Works: Gender Equality By Design* (Boston: Belknap Press, 2016).
12. Michael Lukaszewski, *Streamline: How to Create Healthy Church Systems* (np: Caufield & Finch, 2016), 147.
13. Colin M. Fisher, Julianna Pilemer, and Teresa M. Amabile, "Research: When Help Isn't Helpful" *Harvard Business Review Blog* (June 10, 2025), accessed at https://hbr.org/2025/06/research-when-help-isnt-helpful.
14. Quint Studer, *Results That Last* (Hoboken, NJ: John Wiley & Sons, 2008), 181–183.
15. Donald J. Polden and Barry Z. Posner, *Lawyers as Leaders: Why It Matters and What It Takes* (Chicago: American Bar Association, 2024), 135–136.
16. John Doerr, *Measure What Matters* (New York: Portfolio/Penguin, 2018), 180.
17. Neil Petrie, *Future Trends in Leadership Development* (Greensboro, NC: Center for Creative Leadership, 2014), 17.
18. Marshall Goldsmith, *What Got You Here Won't Get You There* (New York: Hyperion, 2007), 119.
19. Denise Brosseau, *Ready to Be a Thought Leader? How to Increase Your Influence, Impact, and Success* (San Francisco: Jossey-Bass, 2013), 110.

8

Management Still Matters

Many try to make too strong a distinction between leadership and management. In practical application, this forces a false dichotomy. Indeed, a person can be a good manager without being an exceptional leader, and vice versa. Management and leadership admittedly involve different sets of activities, focus areas, and skill sets.

Management: The Art of Getting Things Done is primarily about process, efficiency, and stability. Managers are responsible for planning, organizing, staffing, directing, and controlling resources to achieve specific organizational objectives. For example, a project manager meticulously creates a Gantt chart, assigns specific tasks to team members based on their skills, sets deadlines, monitors progress, and holds regular meetings to ensure the project stays on track and within budget. They address any roadblocks, such as a team member falling behind, by reallocating resources or adjusting the schedule.

Leadership: The Art of Influencing and Inspiring is about vision, inspiration, and change. Leaders motivate and influence people to work toward a common, often long-term, purpose. For instance, during a company-wide town hall, the leader paints a vivid picture of how their new product will revolutionize the industry and improve customers' lives. They share personal anecdotes, convey their passion, and articulate why this endeavor is meaningful, thereby inspiring employees to dedicate themselves to its success, even if it means extra hours or overcoming complex challenges.

While it's been said that managers do things right, and leaders do the right things, when it comes to organizational effectiveness, both are right! Despite their distinct nature, they are rarely effective in complete isolation. For an organization or a team to truly thrive, both elements are crucial. They complement each other, with leadership providing the vision and drive and management providing the structure and control to execute that vision. Not all managers are leaders, and, as well, you don't need to be in a management position to provide leadership.

- *Management Without Leadership:* You can have an individual who is highly skilled at managing resources, adhering to budgets, organizing tasks, and ensuring processes are followed to the letter. They may excel at achieving short-term operational goals, but they might lack the ability to inspire their team, articulate a compelling vision, or navigate significant change. They ensure things run smoothly but might not innovate or motivate beyond compliance.
- *Leadership Without Management:* Conversely, an individual might be incredibly charismatic, visionary, and able to inspire others to a cause. They might be the "idea person" or the "motivational speaker" of a group. However, they might struggle with the practicalities of execution—setting clear deadlines, delegating tasks efficiently, managing budgets, or resolving day-to-day operational issues. Their vision might never materialize without someone (or themselves, if they develop those skills) to manage the concrete steps.

While not strictly required, the presence of both management and leadership is crucial for achieving real-world success, significantly amplifying effectiveness. An organization that emphasizes management alone might be efficient, but it lacks innovation, adaptability, and employee engagement. It might struggle in dynamic environments. An organization that only emphasizes leadership might have inspiring visions but fail to execute them, leading to frustration, chaos, and missed opportunities. The most effective organizations achieve a balance, cultivating both strong managers who also exhibit leadership and empowering leaders at all levels who understand the necessity of structured execution. This balanced approach leads to stability, growth, innovation, and a highly motivated workforce.

> A manager who also possesses strong leadership qualities not only can ensure tasks are completed efficiently but can also motivate their team, foster a positive work environment, encourage innovation within their scope, and help their team understand the "why" behind their work. This leads to higher engagement, better quality, and more proactive problem-solving.

> A leader with management capabilities can translate their grand vision into actionable steps. They can organize the resources, structure the teams, set realistic timelines, and monitor progress, ensuring that their inspiring ideas don't just remain dreams but are successfully executed and realized.

The ideas that management and leadership are distinct yet intertwined, and that one doesn't necessarily require the other (though they greatly enhance each other), are fundamental to understanding organizational effectiveness. Let's delve deeper into these concepts.

The Best Managers Are Also Leaders

This statement highlights the synergy between the two concepts. While management ensures the efficient execution of existing processes, leadership provides the direction and motivation for *what* those processes should achieve and *why*. An effective manager who also possesses leadership qualities can:

- *Communicate the "Why":* Beyond assigning tasks, they can explain the purpose and strategic importance of the work, connecting it to the larger organizational vision.
- *Inspire Their Team:* Instead of simply delegating, they can motivate team members, foster a sense of ownership, and encourage professional growth.

- *Navigate Change:* They can manage the operational aspects of change while also inspiring their team to embrace new approaches.
- *Foster Innovation:* They can create an environment where creativity is encouraged, even within structured processes.

A sales manager not only sets sales targets, monitors performance, and provides coaching (management) but also instills a strong belief in the product's value, inspires the sales team to see themselves as problem-solvers for their clients, and encourages them to constantly seek new ways to connect with customers (leadership). When a new market trend emerges, they don't just adjust quotas; they help the team understand the opportunity, adapt their approach, and feel excited about the challenge.

There is also an abundance of opportunities to provide leadership, without the title of leader or holding some hierarchical (managerial) position. Leadership isn't confined to a job title or a position in the organizational hierarchy. Anyone, at any level, can exhibit leadership by influencing others, taking initiative, and championing a cause. Here are three examples:

- *The Informal Team Lead:* A junior software engineer, without any formal management responsibilities, consistently takes initiative to organize code reviews, mentors new hires, and proposes innovative solutions that improve the team's efficiency. Their colleagues naturally look to them for guidance and follow their suggestions, not because they have to, but because they respect their expertise and judgment.
- *The Subject Matter Expert:* A long-tenured customer service representative, known for their deep understanding of products and customer issues, becomes the go-to person for complex problems. They proactively identify recurring issues, suggest improvements to processes, and informally train their peers,

effectively leading the effort to improve customer satisfaction, even without formal supervisory authority.
- *The Advocate for Change:* An individual contributor notices a significant inefficiency in a company-wide process. They research solutions, develop a compelling presentation, and rally colleagues from different departments to support their proposal, eventually convincing senior management to adopt a new, more effective approach. Their influence stems from their initiative, problem-solving skills, and ability to build consensus, not from holding a management title.

Leaders Must Have Some Degree of Management Competency

While leaders focus on vision and inspiration, their vision cannot be realized without a practical understanding of how to execute. Management competencies are often essential for leaders to translate their strategic ideas into actionable plans. For example:

- *Strategic Planning and Execution:* A C-suite executive develops a bold vision for the company's future, but they must also possess management skills to break down that vision into achievable strategic objectives, allocate resources effectively across departments, set performance metrics, and oversee the implementation of those plans. Without these management competencies, the vision remains an abstract idea.
- *Budgeting and Resource Management:* A nonprofit leader might inspire immense passion for their cause, but to actually deliver on their mission, they need to manage their budget, allocate funds to specific programs, manage staff effectively, and ensure operational efficiency. A compelling vision alone won't feed the hungry or build schools; effective resource management will.
- *Team Organization and Delegation:* A revolutionary entrepreneur (leader) has a groundbreaking idea, but to build a successful

company, they must be able to organize their team, define roles and responsibilities, delegate tasks, and ensure that individuals are held accountable for their contributions. They manage the "how" to achieve their "what."

In conclusion, management and leadership are indeed distinct but complementary. While management focuses on bringing order and efficiency to operations, leadership focuses on setting direction and inspiring people. The most effective individuals, whether in formal management positions or not, seamlessly blend these competencies, recognizing that a clear vision needs structured execution, and efficient processes are far more impactful when driven by a compelling purpose.

Good management skills typically result from a combination of training, experience, and observing how others approach tasks. Management may not be the most glamorous activity for leaders, but it is essential. We learn just how important good management is when it is absent. The greatest of dreams will falter unless leaders pay attention to basic management skills. Some productive areas to develop skills and ask good questions include planning, maximizing the use of meetings, delegation, and time management.

★ ★ ★ ★ ★

Planning

Questions

- Productive planning always requires obtaining good feedback from a range of people involved with your organization. Sometimes, gathering such information from constituents can seem so overwhelming a task that it is not attempted. Verne Harnish, founder of the Entrepreneurs' Organization and CEO coach, offers a simple survey model that can generate valuable insights by using these three questions:

    What do you think we should start doing?

What do you think we should stop doing?

What do you think we should keep doing?[1]

- One of our colleagues worked closely for many years with Walmart's founder Sam Walton. He says that Walton was known to seek out a broad range of opinions and was genuinely interested in the ideas of others. Consequently, you could hear Walton routinely asking people throughout the organization this question:

  What do you think?

- Duke University's Dan Heath points out that multiple people in an organization may regularly face the same problem. This may be due to missing information, something placed in the wrong location, or numerous other factors that result in unnecessary time being spent to rectify the situation. Often, the way leaders discover such issues is by spending time with frontline personnel. Heath encourages leaders to ask people this question:

  Why is it that this keeps happening?[2]

- When leaders are asked about where their visions came from, they often have great difficulty describing the process. When they do provide an answer, typically it's more about a feeling, a sense, a gut reaction, a hunch. What they do have, like the rest of us, are concerns, desires, principles, hypotheses, propositions, arguments, hopes, and dreams—core concepts around which they organize their aspirations and subsequent actions. Visions, write leadership scholars Jim Kouzes and Barry Posner, are projections of your fundamental beliefs and assumptions about human nature, technology, economics, science, politics, art, ethics, and the like. They explain that finding your vision is a process of self-exploration and self-creation, which emerges from asking questions like:

> *What are my fundamental beliefs and assumptions about life and work that keep recurring?*
>
> *What are the themes that keep repeating themselves?*
>
> *What are the social and charitable causes that I contribute to?*
>
> *What are the things that keep me up at night?*
>
> *What are the "I wish" statements that I find myself repeating?*[3]

- Researchers have shown that stressing the "why" to people activates their brain's reward system, subsequently increasing people's efforts and how they feel about what they are doing. Consider the motivational difference between call center employees who see their purpose as helping people solve problems versus those who see their job as getting people off the phone as quickly as possible. People need to know and feel that what they are doing makes a difference. Make sure that you and your team can answer these questions:

> *Why do we do what we do?*
>
> *Why does what we do matter?*[4]

- As part of his turnaround of the morale and performance of an Army community hospital, the colonel in charge needed to enlist people in crafting a shared vision. He organized a retreat for the team, and began by asking them to discuss these three questions:

What are the ideals that attract you to this organization?

What are the higher-order values that give meaning and purpose to your life and work?

Are you in this job to do something, or are you in this job for something to do? If you're here to do something, what is it?[5]

Making the Most of Meetings

Questions

- It's not clear that people "enjoy" meetings, but they can indeed be channels of creativity and productivity if approached thoughtfully. The low expectations that many have when attending meetings testify to the room for improvement. Think of a meeting as a task with a purpose, values, and goals. Too often, meetings are initiated and held regularly, but what would happen if you took a moment to ask people:

  Do we need to meet?

  What is the result we want to achieve from this meeting?

- Since the agendas of many meetings are filled with routine but possibly necessary items, leaders according to client relationships experts Andrew Sobel and Jerold Panas, find it helpful to send this question out to participants to consider before the team or committee is to meet:

  Given our responsibilities, what is the most important thing we should be discussing when we meet next?[6]

- Shaun Ridley, deputy chief executive officer of the Australian Institute of Management (Western Australia), implores leaders to start meetings on time. He maintains that failing to do so infuriates and disrespects those who are on time, reduces the productivity of everyone in attendance, and inflates the sense of self-importance of the latecomer. Ask yourself:

  > *How do I ensure that my meetings start on time?*
  >
  > *How can I prevent backtracking on content when someone is late?*[7]

- You can often discover important issues or uncover key sentiments if you ask questions like these before the meeting concludes (e.g., in the last 5 to 10 minutes):

  > *What is something on your mind that you have not had a chance to say?*
  >
  > *How are you feeling about what we accomplished in this meeting?*
  >
  > *Is there something better we can do in our next meeting?*

- Meetings often generate too many promising ideas. After adequate time to develop a reasonable range of options, you need to focus the conversation by asking questions such as:

  > *Out of all these ideas, which one or two should we emphasize first?*
  >
  > *What would be the logical next steps?*
  >
  > *Who will be responsible for those next steps?*

> *By when can they be done?*
>
> *How will we hold ourselves accountable?*

- Think about wrapping up your meetings by asking a few participants:

  > *What is the big issue, impression, or learning that you are taking away from this meeting?*

- Psychologist and University of North Carolina at Charlotte professor Steven G. Rogelberg says it is important that after a meeting, leaders assess the dynamics. He suggests that if you answer "yes" to all or some of these questions, there is a problem that needs your attention:

  > *Were people distracted?*
  >
  > *Were people conducting side conversations?*
  >
  > *Who did the most talking? Was it you? One or two people?*
  >
  > *Did the discussion stray to irrelevant topics?*
  >
  > *Were all the opinions and ideas that were expressed fairly similar?*[8]

Delegation

Questions

- Being able to delegate is essential because, for one, you can't do everything yourself. The overall efficiency of your team and organization requires getting everyone involved. Doing so also develops the skill level of those around you. Delegation is an art to be cultivated but not abused. Delegation is more than assigning work. You maintain a role as a leader by providing oversight and support along the way. Before delegating, start your thinking process by asking:

> *Who has the skills to do this task well?*
>
> *For whom would this task be a welcome challenge?*

- Doing everything yourself may be efficient but limiting. The following question can help you expand your thinking about the number of people who have the knowledge and ability to do more than they currently do:

> *How might I involve someone else in this project to achieve the task and develop them to assume more responsibility?*

- Effective delegation requires monitoring, but without giving the impression that you do not have confidence in the person assigned to do the task. According to researchers, the following questions may help with check-in conversations along the way:

> *Can you walk me through some of the steps you have taken since our last conversation?*
>
> *How far along is the project today as compared to where you thought it would be?*
>
> *Which steps have been easier or more difficult so far than you had expected?*[9]

- Delegating is difficult for some leaders due to a combination of psychological barriers, practical concerns, and a lack of trust. Often those who were promoted because of their technical prowess, struggle to shift from "doing" to "leading through others." These questions may help you analyze your need for control and the actual cost of doing everything yourself:

    What's the worst-case scenario if this task isn't done exactly my way, and how likely is that to happen?

    How does my doing this task prevent me from focusing on more strategic or impactful work?

    What new and exciting challenges could I take on if I successfully delegated this task?

    What am I gaining by holding onto this task, and what am I losing?

    What part of this task genuinely requires my unique expertise, and what parts could someone else benefit from learning?

    Is this task the best use of my leadership time and skills, given my role?

- Many scholars and authors, like entrepreneur Michael Hyatt, advocate the principle that leaders should delegate tasks even if others will do them only 80% as well as they could themselves. This approach favors momentum over perfection, and it minimizes self-burnout. Consider asking yourself:

    If someone can do this task 80% as well as I can, is that "good enough" to achieve the overall goal?[10]

- Leaders amplify the intelligence of others, what researcher and executive advisor Liz Wiseman calls "multipliers," by asking the right questions and creating space for team growth. Here are several questions to encourage you to assess your team's capabilities and identify areas for development:

  > *What specific skills or knowledge does [Team Member's Name] already possess that are relevant to this task?*
  >
  > *What support or training would [Team Member's Name] need to successfully complete this task?*
  >
  > *What is one small, low-risk task I can delegate to [Team Member's Name] first to build my trust and their confidence?*
  >
  > *How can I set [Team Member's Name] up for success, rather than focusing on potential failure?*
  >
  > *What opportunities for growth or learning would this task provide for [Team Member's Name]?*
  >
  > *If I don't trust my team with this, what steps can I take to build that trust over time?*[11]

- Sometimes, delegation does not work. Should that happen, researchers suggest taking time to ask these questions so that you can better understand what went wrong:

  > *Did I delegate to the wrong person?*
  >
  > *Was the task too much for one person?*
  >
  > *Were my expectations unrealistic?*
  >
  > *Did I provide enough guidance?*
  >
  > *Did I monitor progress and stay connected?*
  >
  > *Was I sufficiently available for support?*[12]

Time Management

Questions

- The Pulitzer Prize winning author Annie Dillard has written that "how we spend our days is, of course, how we spend our lives." Sometimes people speak of this as time management. A better description may be life management. Finding ways for time to align more closely with personal and work goals can bring increased fulfillment and less frustration. Begin this process by asking yourself:

    Am I clear on my top three priorities for today/this week? If not, what's confusing, and how can I gain clarity?

    Did I spend time planning my day before diving into tasks? How effective was that planning, and what could make it better?

    Am I distinguishing between urgent and important tasks? Am I dedicating enough time to the important but not necessarily urgent tasks that drive long-term progress?

    What tasks am I consistently putting off, and why? Is it a lack of clarity, skill, interest, or something else?

- It is easy to accept a new responsibility without considering how much time and effort it involves. Things that seem like relatively modest requests can easily become burdensome when added to an already extensive list of prior commitments. Looking back over the range of such invitations you've accepted during recent months can prepare you to consider this question:

    What types of things can I say "no" to in the future without compromising my goals or effectiveness?

- Just as organizations regularly do program audits to see what still makes sense, you should periodically conduct a personal audit of your various activities with a question such as:

> *Are there things I have done in the past week (or month) that, knowing what I know now, I would not take on again?*

- Robert Greenleaf, whose name is most associated with the concept of servant leadership, said that pacing oneself by appropriate withdrawal is one of the best ways for leaders to make optimal use of their energy and resources. He suggests asking:

> *How can I use myself to serve best?*[13]

- All of us receive frequent requests from others. It is easy to first think, "Should I say yes or no?" Before making that decision, Peter Bregman, considered one of the top leadership coaches in the world, believes you should ask yourself a different set of questions:

> *Am I the right person?*
>
> *Is this the right time?*
>
> *Do I have enough information to decide?*[14]

- If your task list and calendar continue to stay full beyond your capacity to handle it reasonably, then you need to focus and prioritize. Take a hard look at your calendar and to-do list, says simplicity expert Lisa Bodell, and ask yourself:

> *What if I didn't do that?*
>
> *What is the worst that would happen?*[15]

Notes

1. Verne Harnish, *Scaling Up: How a Few Companies Make It . . . and Why the Rest Don't* (Ashburn, VA: Gazelles Inc., 2014), 137.
2. Dan Heath, *Upstream: The Quest to Solve Problems Before They Happen* (New York: Avid Reader Press, 2020), 61.
3. James M. Kouzes and Barry Z. Posner, *The Leadership Challenge: How to Make Extraordinary Things Happen in Organizations*, 7th ed. (Hoboken, NJ: John Wiley & Sons, 2023), 91.
4. Jesse Newton and Josh Davis, "Three Secrets of Organizational Effectiveness," *strategy+business,* Vol. 76, August (2014), reprint 00271.
5. James M. Kouzes and Barry Z. Posner, *op. cit.,* 112.
6. Andrew Sobel and Jerold Panas, *Power Questions Build Relationship, Win New Business, and Influence Others* (Hoboken, NJ: John Wiley & Sons, 2012), 167.
7. Shaun Ridley, *One More Small Step . . . for Leaders: More Practical Actions to Make You a Better Leader Today Than You Were Yesterday* (Floreat, WA: Australian Institute of Management, 2019), 102–103.
8. Steven G. Rogelberg, "Why Your Meetings Stink—and What to Do About It," *Harvard Business Review*, Vol. 97, No. 1 (January–February 2019), 141.
9. Paul Cherry, Patrick Conner, and Karianne Earner-Sparks, *Questions That Get Results* (Hoboken, NJ: John Wiley & Sons, 2011), 35.
10. Michael Hyatt, *Free to Focus: A Total Productivity System to Achieve More by Doing Less* (Ada, MI: Baker Books, 2019).
11. Liz Wiseman, *Multipliers: How the Best Leaders Make Everyone Smarter* (New York: HarperBusiness, 2010).
12. Paul Cherry, Patrick Conner, and Karianne Earner-Sparks, *op. cit.,* 37.
13. Robert K. Greenleaf, *Servant Leadership* (New York: Paulist Press, 1977), 19.
14. Peter Bregman, *18 Minutes: Find Your Focus, Master Distraction, and Get the Right Things Done* (New York: Business Plus, 2011), 189.
15. Lisa Bodell, *Why Simple Wins* (Brookline, MA: Bibliomotion, 2017), 171.

9
Communication

Leaders should see themselves as the chief communication officers for their organizations. Generous communication in all directions and through multiple means inspires commitment to overall goals. Good leaders remind everyone of the purpose, goals, and values of the organization and how important each person is to achieving goals.

You need to give the time and care to such communication that is required because much is at stake. According to the Harris Poll and Grammarly Business 2023 *The State of Business Communication*, the majority of business leaders and knowledge workers believe that effective communication is "key to business performance."[1] It enhances productivity, improves collaboration, and powers up work experiences.

Effective leadership is about developing and nurturing your relationships with others. The very best leaders connect with people and have high-quality relationships with them. The one thing that any leader can do that will make them more effective, according to Professor Ron Riggio, former director of the Kravis Leadership Institute at Claremont McKenna College, is "improve communications."[2]

Leaders play a pivotal role in fostering effective communication within an organization. To improve communications, leaders should regularly ask themselves and their teams a series of critical questions.

These questions can be broadly categorized into self-reflection, making connections, and listening.

★ ★ ★ ★ ★

Self-Reflection

Questions

- Leaders are constantly striving to improve, and communication is often cited as a key area for development. One place to begin is by reflecting on your interactions with others. For example, when this mid-level manager told us that lately their team meetings seemed off, flat, without much energy, we asked him to say more about why he felt this way:

    On reflection, I realize I dominated the conversation, especially when we discussed the new project timeline. I was so focused on conveying the urgency and my own ideas that I probably cut off Sonia twice when she tried to offer a different perspective. That's a bad habit I need to break. My body language probably didn't help either—I tend to lean forward intensely when I'm stressed, which can come across as aggressive, not just engaged.

    We asked him to think about what he might have done differently:

    I didn't explicitly ask for feedback on my proposal, assuming everyone was on board. That's a huge oversight. True communication isn't just about transmitting information; it's about ensuring understanding and fostering dialogue. I need to intentionally create space for others to speak, even if it means pausing and asking direct questions like, "What are your initial thoughts?" or "Does anyone have concerns or alternative approaches?"

Like this manager, there are several things you need to think about in your interactions and communications with others:

Am I listening more than talking?

Am I actively listening and seeking to understand, or just waiting for my turn to speak?

Am I truly hearing what my team members are saying?

Am I inviting diverse opinions?

Am I using open-ended questions?

Am I approachable and accessible to my team?

Do people feel comfortable coming to me with questions or concerns?

- In reflecting on how well you communicate, consider asking yourself both broad and concrete questions, such as:

Am I clear and concise in my messages? Do I use jargon or overly complex language when simpler terms would suffice?

Do I tailor my message to my audience? Am I considering their background, knowledge, and what they need to know?

Do I ensure understanding, or do I just assume it?

How do I check for comprehension (e.g., asking open-ended questions, having them paraphrase)?

Are my expectations clear? Do my team members know exactly what's expected of them, their roles, and desired outcomes?

- Empathy is a critical component of effective communication, particularly in leadership and professional contexts according to William Gentry, senior research scientist at the Center for Creative Leadership. It fosters understanding, builds trust, and improves relationships. Think about how well you demonstrate empathy in your communications:

    Do I consider the emotional impact of my messages on others?

    Do I connect with my team members on a human level, beyond just tasks and deliverables?

    Do I acknowledge and validate others' perspectives, even if I disagree with them?

    Am I approachable and accessible? Do my team members feel comfortable coming to me with questions or concerns?[3]

- Considering communication channels and ensuring consistency are fundamental to effective communication, as they improve the quality of understanding and help to keep everyone on the same page. Cerkl Broadcast, a company specializing in internal communications, contends: "To ensure the success of vision alignment messaging, consistency is key. Leaders need to be clear and direct and relay the messages repeatedly to all employees, including frontline workers. The use of various communication tools like meetings, email communications, and visual presentations can make the delivery more effective." Accordingly, you need to set aside some time to contemplate:

    Am I using the most effective communication channels for different types of messages (e.g., in-person for sensitive topics, email for general updates, instant messaging for quick queries)?

Am I communicating consistently across the organization?

Are there conflicting messages coming from different sources?

Do I over-communicate or under-communicate?

Am I providing the right amount of information at the right time?

How often do I communicate critical information, and is it shared broadly enough?

Making Connections

Questions

Making connections with others through communications is about building rapport, understanding, and trust beyond just the exchange of information. It involves a genuine interest in the other person and a willingness to be vulnerable and open. Here are several examples:

- During a one-on-one meeting, the leader, Lynn, wants to get to know a new team member, Emily, beyond her résumé, and asks: "Emily, beyond your immediate project tasks, what are you most excited about learning or developing in your role here? Or, what's a challenge you're currently grappling with that you're passionate about solving?"
- The leader, Steve, recalls a casual conversation a week ago where a team member, Chloe, mentioned her child was feeling unwell. The next time he sees Chloe, Steve might say, "Hey Chloe, I hope you don't mind me asking, but how is your daughter doing? Is she feeling any better?"
- A team member, Sara, approaches her leader, David, appearing stressed and anxious about a project deadline. Instead of immediately jumping into solutions, David leans in, maintains eye contact, and says, "Sara, I can see you're really feeling the pressure about this deadline. Let me know what's on your mind.

I'm here to listen." He then allows Sara to fully express her concerns without interruption, occasionally nodding or saying, "I understand," to show he's engaged. He might then follow up with, "It sounds like you're worried about X and Y. Is that right?" to confirm his understanding.

- A team successfully completes a challenging mini-project ahead of schedule. In addition to a general "Great job, team," the team's leader, Carlos, might say, "Fantastic work on the analytics dashboard, everyone!" Especially to Liam, "I know you pulled some late nights to get that data validated, and it really paid off." And to Emma, "Your presentation was incredibly clear and concise—really highlighted the key insights."

★ ★ ★ ★ ★

- Communication consultant Michael Sheehan says that leaders, as they anticipate a speaking responsibility, often begin by thinking about "What do I want to say?" which he maintains is the wrong question. The more useful question, but one that usually cannot be answered quickly, is:

  What do I want to accomplish?[4]

- In communicating ideas to others, it is easy to frame the message based on what you know instead of what the audience is interested in learning. This question can help you think about connecting with the interests of your audience:

  If I were in their places, what would I want to know?

  What does my audience want to take away from my remarks?

- Decisions are routinely made by staff and committees about matters rightfully in their domains of responsibility. Just as often, while the logistics of the change go smoothly, the fallout from those unaware of the pending change and its rationale can negatively impact morale and productivity. When a change is planned, it is crucial to be sure to ask questions such as:

With whom do we need to consult to make sure this change can work?

Who else needs to be notified of the change?

- Nothing disrupts successful change more than a lack of adequate communication and clear information. Peter Drucker, the influential management thinker, says that in anticipation of any change, no matter how minor, you should ask the following question:

  Who needs to be informed about this?

- Maxine Fears, logistics coordinator at Impact Church in Atlanta, has several questions in mind when any group brings forward an idea for a new program or project. Among her questions are:

  Who will be affected by this?

  Who needs to be involved for this to be a success?

  What is the best way to communicate with each of these people?

- Good leaders spend considerable time listening and observing and thus learn a great deal about problems and possibilities. The next step, rather than telling people, "Here is the situation, and this is what we need to do," is to say, "Thank you for sharing your time and ideas so generously to help me understand how things are. Now, I need some additional help. I want to share what I'm hearing from you and ask you a few questions."

> *Does what I'm saying match your observations?*
>
> *Am I hearing things correctly?*
>
> *Did I miss something?*

- Someone asks to talk with you on a topic about which you know a great deal. The conversation could easily start with you telling them everything you know, rather than finding out what aspect of what you know is most needed by the person coming to visit with you. A question that focuses the conversation on the needs of the other person is:

> *What outcome would make this conversation a success for you?*

Listening

Questions

Listening is not merely the absence of speaking; it's a fundamental and active component of being a truly effective communicator and leader. While many equate good communication with speaking clearly or persuasively, the ability to listen profoundly impacts how well your messages are received, understood, and acted upon. Consider the difference in outcomes when there is a lack of listening versus one that involves active listening. Here's the scenario: Cathy, the project manager, is meeting with her team member, Andrew, who seems overwhelmed.

Andrew: *Cathy, I'm really struggling with the new client presentation. I've spent hours on it, but I can't seem to get the data to align, and I'm worried about the client's reaction.*

Cathy (interrupting, not truly listening): *Andrew, you just need to power through it. The client expects excellence, and we don't have time for delays. Have you tried the template I created? It's always worked for me. Just follow that. We need this by the end of the day.*

The **outcome** is that Andrew feels unheard, unsupported, and even more stressed. He doesn't feel comfortable sharing his specific difficulties or asking for help. He might try to "power through" but will likely produce a subpar presentation, or work late into the night, leading to burnout. Communication has broken down.

Andrew: *Cathy, I'm really struggling with the new client presentation. I've spent hours on it, but I can't seem to get the data to align, and I'm worried about the client's reaction.*

Cathy (listening attentively, maintaining eye contact, nodding): *Thanks for bringing this to my attention, Andrew. I can see you're feeling a lot of pressure. When you say, 'the data won't align,' can you elaborate a bit on what specific challenge you're encountering? Is it a technical issue, or are you having trouble interpreting certain figures?*

Andrew: *Well, it's actually both. The latest sales figures from Q1 conflict with the marketing forecast for Q2, and I'm not sure which set of numbers to prioritize for the client's strategic goals.*

Cathy (listening, then responding thoughtfully): *Ah, I see. That's a critical point, and it's good you caught that discrepancy. It sounds like you're trying to figure out the narrative for the client given those conflicting figures. Instead of trying to force them to align, perhaps we need to address the discrepancy directly with the client or get clarification from the sales and marketing leads. Let's look at those numbers together for 15 minutes right now. We can then decide the best approach. And don't worry about the deadline until we've got a clear plan.*

The **outcome**: Andrew feels understood, supported, and relieved. Cathy's active listening allowed her to pinpoint the *actual* problem (conflicting data interpretation, not just a struggle with the presentation format). By listening, she could offer a relevant, targeted solution (reviewing data, clarifying strategy) rather than a generic one. This builds trust, strengthens their working relationship, and ultimately leads to a better presentation and a more confident team member.

In this example, Cathy's listening skills transformed a moment of struggle into an opportunity for effective collaboration and problem-solving, demonstrating her leadership and communication prowess.

★ ★ ★ ★ ★

- When a leader actively listens, it signals to people that their thoughts, concerns, and ideas are valued. This creates an environment of *psychological safety*, where individuals feel comfortable speaking up without fear of judgment or reprisal. Harvard Business School Professor Amy Edmondson, famous for pioneering this concept, offers these questions to gauge and explore how people are feeling with one another:

  > *On a scale of 1 to 10, how comfortable do you feel taking a risk or making a mistake on this team? (Follow up with "Why?")*
  >
  > *Do you feel safe to offer your opinion, even if it goes against the majority or my opinion?*
  >
  > *When we make a mistake, do we learn from it collectively, or do we tend to look for someone to blame?*
  >
  > *Do you feel comfortable asking for help when you're stuck or unsure?*
  >
  > *If you had a concern about a project or a team member's approach, how confident are you that it would be heard and addressed constructively?*
  >
  > *What could we do as a team to make it safer for everyone to share ideas and concerns?*[5]

- Listening goes beyond just hearing words; it involves understanding the full message, including nonverbal cues and underlying emotions. A leader who listens attentively can grasp the nuances of a situation, identify root causes of problems, and uncover innovative solutions. By genuinely listening to the specifics, you can then identify targeted training needs, advocate for software improvements, or address workflow inefficiencies, leading to more effective problem-solving and better outcomes for the team and the organization. Consider listening carefully, explains organizational psychologist Roger Schwarz, to people's responses to questions like:

> *Can you explain that in a different way?*
>
> *What specifically do you mean by [key term or phrase]?*
>
> *Can you give me an example of what that looks like in practice?*
>
> *What do you believe is the core problem we're trying to solve here?*
>
> *What are all the possible causes of this problem?*
>
> *What are some different ways we could approach this?*
>
> *If we tried [proposed solution], what might be the potential challenges or unintended consequences?*[6]

- You need to appreciate that one person may have a valid point of view about a problem, but individuals from different backgrounds can offer diverse perspectives on the same problem. The extra information and varied perspectives can help you formulate better answers and improve outdated systems. Successful leaders need to encourage the sharing of information from all stakeholders, be receptive to different ideas no matter the source, and use the collective knowledge to develop an effective solution to any challenge. Some thoughtful questions you can ask yourself are:

  > *What perspectives are currently missing from this conversation?*
  >
  > *Who else should be at the table to help us better understand this issue?*

> *How do we ensure that people from different backgrounds feel safe sharing their views?*
>
> *What mechanisms do we have for gathering input from all stakeholders?*
>
> *How can we use feedback from diverse voices to improve our current processes?*

- Becoming better leaders and communicators involves the ability to listen not to just yourself (insight) but to expand your "outsight," which consists of learning from doing—the insight you gain from action, particularly by stepping outside your comfort zone, trying new things, interacting beyond your usual circles, and exposing yourself to different contexts and ideas. Researchers find that unless people actively encourage external communication and seek diverse points of view, they tend to interact with outsiders less and less frequently and subsequently find themselves cut off from new ideas.[7] To keep from falling into this trap, London Business School Professor Herminia Ibarra suggests that you ask yourself questions along these lines:

> *What's one new activity, role, or challenge I can take on that stretches my leadership boundaries?*
>
> *Who in my organization (or outside it) is doing something completely different, and what can I learn from them?*
>
> *When was the last time I worked on something I wasn't already good at?*
>
> *Who do I rarely talk to that might offer a fresh perspective on our current challenge?*
>
> *How can I spend more time with people outside my function, sector, or discipline?*
>
> *What networks or communities am I not part of—but should be?*[8]

- Leaders need to know that what others are feeling is important. It is through understanding their constituents, listening to them, and taking their advice that leaders can give voice to their constituents' feelings and aspirations. You want to be able to stand before others and say with assurance, "Here's what I heard you say that you want for yourselves. Here's how enlisting in our common cause will serve your needs and interests." Consider this experience of a marketing manager for a cloud-based software company shared by leadership scholars Jim Kouzes and Barry Posner:

  I began to actively and deeply listen to people. I started a collaborative, open environment to promote the free exchange of ideas. In turn, people began opening up with one another and actively talking about substantive improvements that they felt could be made to the organization as a whole. I started meeting individually with each of them, asking questions about what they thought were the key issues and best alternatives, and incorporating their feedback into our decisions. I asked people what they were proud of, what brought them to work every day, what management was doing well, and where they were blowing it.

  More importantly, once I asked the questions, I stopped and focused directly on the person answering. I found at first that some people were startled by the attention. After a few tries, though, the level of response and the value of those responses in contributing to defining a vision for our team grew immeasurably. I also began spending more time going out and visiting my employees' and colleagues' workspaces. This increase in interaction allowed me to benefit from their varied perspectives and further enabled us to craft a vision that we can call our own.

- If you don't listen, you will quickly find yourself surrounded by people who have nothing to say, and you know that's seldom true. By asking questions and, crucially, actively listening to their responses, like the marketing manager in the above example did, you can facilitate powerful conversations that uncover common ground and forge a compelling, shared vision that motivates and unites your team. What do people say to you when you ask them:

> *What values do you believe are most essential for us to uphold as a team/organization?*
>
> *What do you believe is our greatest strength as a team/organization right now?*
>
> *What kind of impact should we want to have on our customers/community/stakeholders?*
>
> *Imagine we're wildly successful in [specific timeframe, e.g., five years]. What does that look like? What have we accomplished?*
>
> *What core principles or beliefs should guide us as we pursue this vision?*
>
> *How can we ensure this vision genuinely reflects all of our perspectives?*[9]

Notes

1. Harris Poll and Grammarly Business, *The State of Business Communication: New Threats and Opportunities* [Report] (Harris Poll; Grammarly Business 2023, February 21).
2. Ronald E. Riggio, *Daily Leadership Development: 365 Steps to Becoming a Better Leader* (Thousand Oaks, CA: Sage Publications, 2020), 319.
3. William Gentry, *Be the Boss Everyone Wants to Work For: A Guide for New Leaders* (Oakland, CA: Berrett-Koehler Publishers, 2016).
4. Jennifer Reingold, "The Man Behind the Curtain," *Fast Company*, Vol. 104 (October 2004), 104.

5. Amy Edmondson, *The Fearless Organization: Creating Psychological Safety in the Workplace for Learning, Innovation, and Growth* (Hoboken, NJ: John Wiley & Sons, 2018).
6. Roger Schwarz, *The Skilled Facilitator: A Comprehensive Resource For Consultants, Facilitators, Coaches, and Trainers,* 3rd ed. (San Francisco: Jossey-Bass, 2018).
7. For example, Robert S. Huckman, Bradley R. Staats, and David M. Upton, "Team Familiarity, Role Experience, and Performance: Evidence from Indian Software Services," *Management Science* (2009), *55*(1), 85–100; and Gervase R. Bushe and Alexandra Chu, "Fluid Teams: Solutions to the Problems of Unstable Team Membership," *Organizational Dynamics* (2011), *40*(3), 181–188.
8. Herminia Ibarra, *Act Like a Leader, Think Like a Leader* (Boston: Harvard Business Review Press, 2015).
9. James M. Kouzes and Barry Z. Posner, *The Leadership Challenge: How to Make Extraordinary Things Happen in Organizations*, 7th ed. (Hoboken, NJ: John Wiley & Sons, 2023), 103.

10
Making a Difference

The intent and aspiration of leaders is to make a difference. That's part of the challenge of life, regardless of where you are in an organization or whatever it is you are doing. It's a specific responsibility of those in positions of responsibility, especially for "getting work accomplished through others" (an often-shorthand definition of leadership). Leaders have the opportunity to guide, motivate, set agendas, and make life better for many people. The most effective and influential leaders think beyond what is required by their job descriptions and dream of how things can be better because of their efforts.

Years ago, executive coach Tae Moon Kouzes, told us that every leader she had ever worked with wanted to leave a legacy. Leadership scholars and authors Jim Kouzes and Barry Posner report that the theme of legacy runs through the majority of the lessons they have learned from leaders over the years. They write in their book *A Leader's Legacy* that:

> *Thinking about a legacy can be extremely energizing and uplifting. It forces us to think about today's actions in a larger context.*

It requires an appreciation of others . . . It requires us to take responsibility for our own actions with a realization that they will have consequences, if not immediately, then for sure in the future. The legacy perspective explicitly reveals that we make a difference. Then the only question remaining to consider is, What kind of difference do I want to make?[1]

Few of us, including leaders especially, ever lack for things to do. Seldom do we come to the end of the day without a list of unfinished tasks. Without focusing, leaders would be on a constant treadmill of duties, expectations, and goals. Like Sisyphus, they would be condemned by the gods to an eternal punishment, rolling a massive boulder up a hill, only for it to roll back down each time they neared the top.

Learning to set priorities is equally important for individuals and organizations. Many things may be good, even important, but not all are of equal potential for producing positive results. Some may be worthwhile, but the timing is not correct. And other challenges and opportunities may simply not fit with your skills and resources. The measure of leaders and groups is not how hard they work but how what they do makes a difference.

★ ★ ★ ★ ★

Purpose

Questions

- Identifying your purpose is critically important, personally and as a leader, because it provides the foundation for authenticity, direction, and resilience. When you know your "why," you can make clearer decisions, aligning your values and actions, and set meaningful goals. Being clear about your purpose enables you to prioritize what matter the most amid competing demands and tempting distractions. Bill George, former CEO of Medtronic, refers to this as "discovering your true north." How would you answer these questions?

What kind of impact do I want to have?

When do I feel most alive and effective?

What values guide my decisions, even under pressure?

If I stepped away tomorrow, what legacy would I hope to leave?[2]

- Credibility is built on a foundation of acting with integrity, aligning actions with your espoused values, and according to scholars, is how you build trust with colleagues, followers, and stakeholders. How would you respond to these questions:

What are my five most important values?

What do I believe when it comes to people and relationships?

In retrospect, have I made the right trade-offs between competing values?

Can I live with myself doing what the organization asks of me?

Have I made promises that I cannot realistically fulfill? What should I do if there is a disconnect?

Am I comfortable being my genuine self with my team, including admitting when I don't have all the answers?[3]

- John Izzo and Jeff VanderWielen advocate that companies have a meaning and purpose beyond just profit-making. Purpose-driven leaders engage and motivate people most effectively. When a leader communicates a genuine, compelling purpose, people feel they're working for something larger than themselves, not just a paycheck. In turbulent times, people especially seek meaningful work, and a leader's clarity of purpose helps align individual contributions with a greater mission. With a clear sense of purpose, you are more likely to engage in lifelong learning, seek feedback, and grow intentionally, because you know what you're growing toward. What do you say when others ask you these questions:

> *How does your personal purpose connect with the overarching purpose of this organization?*
>
> *Beyond immediate goals, what long-term impact do you genuinely want to have on people, the organization, and broader community?*
>
> *How does this desired impact influence strategic planning and daily priorities?*
>
> *How are you effectively articulating this long-term vision to inspire, engage, and align the team?*[4]

Intentionality

Questions

- While metrics are critical for leadership, there is always debate about whether we are measuring the right things. Andy Grove, one of Intel's founders, used two questions to determine what his company should measure:

> *Where do we want to go?*
>
> *How will we know we're getting there?*[5]

- Peter Drucker pointed out that throughout history, the great majority of people never had to ask the question, "What should I contribute?" They were told what to contribute. Today, many people have choices about not only what work they do but what they hope to achieve through their lives. Drucker said people need to answer the question, "What should my contribution be?" To gain insight into your contribution, he suggested these three questions:

  What does the situation require?

  Given my strengths, my way of performing, and my values, how can I make the most significant contribution to what needs to be done?

  What results must be achieved to make a difference?[6]

- Beginning a new venture is always exciting. Researchers offer two good questions for groups to keep in mind and ground themselves before launching any new effort:

  Are initiatives being launched without success metrics?

  Is the success of this initiative being evaluated primarily by the leaders who launched and own the project?[7]

- You will need to focus if you intend to offer or produce a distinctive contribution. In his book *Essentialism*, which is not about how to get more things done; it's about how to get the right stuff done, Greg McKeown provides two questions that can help with this:

  If we could be truly excellent at only one thing, what would it be?

  How will we know when we have succeeded?[8]

- This is a simple question (not that the answer to it, mind you, is simple) that you may find helpful to ask at the beginning of the week:

  > *Of all the things on which I am working this week, which one will make the most difference a year or longer from now?*

- Organizations can often contribute to the lack of leadership by keeping everyone so busy putting out fires that there's little time left to consider fire prevention measures. Find ways to keep yourself from being so caught up in daily tasks that days or weeks go by without giving attention to what is the biggest goal or challenge facing you. Asking this question each morning may give you some direction:

  > *Given my big goal for this year, what will I do toward that goal today?*

- Do you have a "big goal for the year?" As an alternative to determining, "What's most important?" identify a "wildly important goal" by asking this question:

  > *If every other area of our operation remained at its current level of performance, what is the one area where change would have the most significant impact?*[9]

- When ideas are requested in a meeting, leaders want to affirm all contributions, but sometimes some suggestions may seem irrelevant or unconnected to the question at hand. When this is your sense, it may be a good time to ask:

  > *Can you say more about how you see your idea contributing to our goal?*

The Leader's Role

Questions

- Leaders live with a constant flurry of activities, demands, and expectations on top of the ever-expanding "to-do" list they bring to their work each week. It is no wonder that important major goals can be neglected. One way to lead the big challenges and opportunities, even in the busiest of times, is to have this question on the top of your mind:

  What is one thing I can do to advance [the goal] today (or this week)?

- Most leaders do not find it hard to stay busy. The challenge is to identify those things that you can do that are most important to be done. Discover one key category of critical tasks by asking yourself, says leadership coach Scott Eblin:

  What is it that—given the perspective and resources I have [in this position]—only I can do?[10]

- Finding time for life's priorities is always a challenge. Ask yourself this question to help make sure you have carved out some time for what matters most:

  To what can I say "no" to so that I can say "yes" to something more important?

- Gain greater clarity and control over your time, and consistently invest in what truly matters by periodically recalibrating. For example, consider what to do with your answer to this question:

  Am I letting others' priorities dictate my urgency, or am I setting my own?

- Stephen Covey's core idea, famously presented in his book *The 7 Habits of Highly Effective People*, is that our effectiveness stems from how we choose to spend our time, specifically by distinguishing between what is urgent and what is important (or essential). He argues that most people mistakenly focus on urgency, leading to a life of constant reaction and crisis management, rather than proactive, meaningful work. Ask yourself:

In which quadrant(s) am I currently operating the most?

Q1: Urgent/Important

Q2: Not Urgent/Important

Q3: Urgent/Not Important

Q4: Not Urgent/Not Important?[11]

- Once you have identified where you are spending most of your time according to Covey's 2 × 2 matrix, here are some questions to ask about your overall time management, focus, and effectiveness:

How much time do I spend in Quadrant 1 (Crises)? What are the recurring crises, and what proactive steps could I take to move them into Quadrant 2 (prevention)?

How much time am I currently investing in Quadrant 2 (Important/Not Urgent)? What would happen if I doubled that time?

What am I currently doing in Quadrant 3 (Urgent/Not Important)? Who or what is driving these "urgent" demands that don't align with my priorities?
How can I delegate, decline, or compartmentalize them?

What am I doing in Quadrant 4 (Not Urgent/Not Important)? How much time is truly wasted, and what value does it bring (or not bring)?

- Maintaining your focus on Q2 (Important/Not Urgent) matters necessitates asking questions such as:

    What's one Q2 activity I could re-arrange and schedule for tomorrow or next week with little consequence?

    How can I better protect my time for Q2 activities from interruptions and distractions?

    What system or routine can I implement to consistently integrate more Q2 activities into my week?

    If I only had [X amount of time, e.g., 2 hours] each day, what Q2 activities would I prioritize?

- Deciding whether to sit still and hold on to what you are doing or pursue a new opportunity and take on more commitments is a challenge for all of us, and especially leaders. To help make this determination, best-selling author Greg McKeown offers two questions to consider:

    Can I actually fulfill this request, given the time and resources I have?

    Is this the very most important thing I should be doing with my time and resources right now?[12]

- Times of transition are occasions of great opportunity and risk. Mistakes are easily made in these times as standard practices and relationships prove inadequate or inappropriate. Transitions are challenging for both leaders and organizations undergoing change. Often, the tasks associated with transition overshadow the emotional and spiritual dimensions that accompany change—dimensions that are crucial to navigating any transition. When you consider accepting a new position (or even a new major assignment), asking these questions will help provide some clarity about what you are getting yourself into:

> *What is the purpose of this position? Why does it exist?*
>
> *What are the outcomes expected of this position?*
>
> *What are the responsibilities and tasks of this position?*
>
> *How does this position fit into the larger organization?*

- A useful question for anyone making a move or taking on a new position is:

> *How will I establish my network of support in my new location or role?*

- At their last board meeting of the year, one nonprofit organization asks its members to record their individual answers to this question (although this could be adapted at any level or with any group or organization). They discuss the responses in small groups before debriefing and then work to reach consensus as a total group:

> *As we approach a new year, what advice do you have for our board to be even more effective this next year?*
>
> *What advice do you have for our executive director?*

Notes

1. James M. Kouzes and Barry Z. Posner, *A Leader's Legacy* (San Francisco: Jossey-Bass, 2006), 4.
2. Bill George, *Discover Your True North* (New York: The Times Group Book, 2015).

3. James M. Kouzes and Barry Z. Posner, *Credibility: How Leaders Gain and Lose It, Why People Demand It*, 2nd ed. (Hoboken, NJ: John Wiley & Sons, 2011).
4. John B. Izzo and Jeff VanderWielen, *The Purpose Revolution: How Leaders Create Engagement And Competitive Advantage In An Age Of Social Good* (Oakland, CA: Berrett-Koehler Publishers, 2018).
5. Salim Ismail, *Exponential Organizations* (New York: Diversion Books, 2014), 92.
6. Peter F. Drucker, "Managing Oneself," *Harvard Business Review*, Vol. 83, No. 1 (January 2005), 106.
7. Rose Hollister and Michael D. Watkins, "Too Many Projects," *Harvard Business Review*, Vol. 96, No. 5 (September–October 2018), 69.
8. Greg McKeown, *Essentialism: The Disciplined Pursuit of Less* (New York: Crown Business, 2014), 127–128.
9. Cathy McChesney, Sean Covey, and Jim Huling, *The 4 Disciplines of Execution: Achieving Your Wildly Important Goals* (New York: Free Press, 2012), 32.
10. Scott Eblin, *The Next Level: What Insiders Know About Executive Success* 2nd ed. (Boston: Nicholas Brealey America, 2010).
11. Stephen R. Covey, *The 7 Habits of Highly Effective People: Powerful Lessons in Personal Change* (New York: Free Press, 2006).
12. Greg McKeown, *op. cit.*, 2.

Suggested Reading

You ask, "Is there more?"

Yes, there is, and we gratefully acknowledge the great contributions that others have made to helping people get to the best answers. Here are some excellent resources to consult and learn more about questions, their significance, and their application:

- Adams, Marilee G., *Change Your Questions, Change Your Life: 12 Powerful Tools for Leadership, Coaching, and Life*, 4th ed. (Oakland, CA: Berrett-Koehler Publishers, 2022).
- Berger, Warren, *A More Beautiful Question: The Power of Inquiry to Spark Breakthrough Ideas* (Bloomsbury USA, 2016).
- Berson, Alan S., and Stieglitz, Richard G., *Leadership Conversations: Challenging High-Potential Managers to Become Great Leaders* (San Francisco: Jossey-Bass, 2013).
- Besieux, Tina, "The Art of Asking Great Questions." *Harvard Business Review* (2022, May 17). Retrieved at https://hbr.org/2022/05/the-art-of-asking-great-questions.
- Brooks, Alison Woods, and John, Leslie K., "The Surprising Power of Questions," *Harvard Business Review*, 96(3), 60–67 (2018, May–June).

- Cherry, Paul, Conner, Patrick, and Earner-Sparks, Karianne, *Questions That Get Results* (Hoboken, NJ: John Wiley & Sons, 2011).
- Cohen, Gary B., *Just Ask Leadership: Why Great Managers Always Ask the Right Questions* (New York, NY: McGraw-Hill, 2009).
- Falone, Paul, *101 Tough Conversations to Have with Employees: A Manager's Guide to Addressing Performance, Conduct, and Discipline Challenges* (New York: HarperCollins, 2019).
- Fadem, Terry J., *The Art of Asking: Ask Better Questions, Get Better Answers* (Upper Saddle River, NJ: Financial Times Press, 2009).
- Grazer, Brian, *A Curious Mind: The Secret to a Bigger Life* (New York: Simon & Schuster, 2015).
- Gregersen, Hal, "Bursting the CEO Bubble: Why Executives Should Talk Less and Ask More Questions," *Harvard Business Review*, 95(2), 94–103 (2017, March–April).
- Gregersen, Hal, *Questions Are the Answer: A Breakthrough Approach to Your Most Vexing Problems at Work and in Life* (New York: Harper Business, 2018).
- Johnson, Steven, *Where Good Ideas Come From: The Natural History of Innovation* (New York: Riverhead, 2010).
- Leeds, Dorothy, *The Seven Powers of Questions* (New York: Perigee, 2000).
- Lotardo, Elizabeth, "Stop Solving Your Team's Problems for Them," *Harvard Business Review*, (2025, July 14). Retrieved from https://hbr.org/2022/05/the-art-of-asking-great-questions.
- McKeown, George, *Essentialism: The Disciplined Pursuit of Less* (New York: Crown Business, 2014).
- Marquardt, Michael J. and Tiede, Bob, *Leading with Questions: How Leaders Discover Powerful Answers by Knowing How and What to Ask* (Hoboken, NJ: John Wiley & Sons, 2023).
- Saxton, Juliette, Miller, Carole, Laidlaw, Linda, & O'Mara, Joanne, *Asking Better Questions: Teaching and Learning for a Changing World* (3rd ed.) (Pembroke Publishers Limited, 2018).
- Schein, Edgar H., *Humble Inquiry: The Gentle Art of Asking Instead of Telling* (Oakland CA: Berrett-Koehler Publishers, 2013).

- Scott, Kim, *Radical Candor: Be a Kick-Ass Boss Without Losing Your Humanity* (New York: St. Martin's Press, 2019).
- Sesno, Frank, *Ask More: The Power of Questions to Open Doors, Uncover Solutions, and Spark Change* (New York: AMACOM, 2023).
- Sobel, Andrew, and Panas, Jerold, *Power Questions Build Relationship, Win New Business, and Influence Others* (Hoboken, NJ: John Wiley & Sons, 2012).
- Stanier, Michael Bungay, *The Coaching Habit: Say Less, Ask More & Change the Way You Lead Forever* (Vancouver, BC: Page Two, 2016).
- Strachan, Dorothy, *Making Questions Work: A Guide to How and What to Ask for Facilitators, Consultants, Managers, Coaches, and Educators* (San Francisco: Jossey-Bass, 2006).
- Wise, Will, and Littlefield, Chad. *Ask Powerful Questions: Create Conversations That Matter* (CreateSpace Independent Publishing Platform, 2017).

About the Authors

Barry Z. Posner, PhD, is the Michael J. Accolti, S.J. Professor of Leadership at Santa Clara University and Chair of the Management and Entrepreneurship Department. His tenure at Santa Clara University includes 4,386 days as Dean of the Leavey School of Business. Barry's academic contributions have been recognized with numerous awards, including the Association for Talent Development's highest honor for Distinguished Contribution to Workplace Learning and Performance. He has been acknowledged as one of America's Top 50 leadership coaches, ranked among the Most Influential HR Thinkers globally by *HR* magazine and the World's Top 75 Leadership and Management Experts by *Inc.* magazine.

He is the co-author, with Jim Kouzes, of the award-winning and best-selling leadership book *The Leadership Challenge*. It is listed among the Top 100 Business Books of All Time, receiving book-of-the-year honors by the American Council of Health Care Executives and *Fast Company* and the Critic's Choice Award from the nation's book review editors. Barry has co-authored other award-winning, inspiring, and practical books on leadership: *Lawyers as Leaders: What It Takes and Why It Matters*; *Everyday People, Extraordinary Leadership: How to Make a*

Difference Regardless of Your Title, Role, or Authority; Leadership in Higher Education: Practices That Make a Difference; Stop Selling & Start Leading; Learning Leadership: The Five Fundamentals for Becoming an Exemplary Leader; Credibility: How Leaders Gain and Lose It, Why People Demand It; The Truth About Leadership: The No-Fads, Heart-of-the Matter Facts You Need to Know; Encouraging the Heart: Igniting Purpose and Providing Meaningful Recognition; A Leader's Legacy; and *The Student Leadership Challenge.*

Barry has served on the board of the American Institute of Architects, Center for Excellence in Nonprofits, Global Women's Leadership Network, Sigma Phi Epsilon Fraternity, SVCreates, Uplift Family Services, and the Berkeley Food Network. He has delivered presentations and conducted workshops throughout the United States and worldwide. He can be reached directly at bposner@scu.edu.

Lovett H. Weems, Jr., is a senior consultant with the Lewis Center for Church Leadership and a Distinguished Professor of Church Leadership at Wesley Theological Seminary in Washington, DC. Lovett was the founding director of the Lewis Center in 2003, having previously served for 18 years as president of Saint Paul School of Theology in Kansas City, Missouri. A native of Mississippi, he was a pastor in that state for many years. His years in Mississippi were marked by an emphasis on both church leadership and public issues. His work in Mississippi led the distinguished Mississippi writer Willie Morris to describe him as "one of the persons who added much to the growing civility of Mississippi."

Lovett is the author of many books on church leadership that have had a broad appeal to a large constituency of leaders in both the public and private sectors. His influential book, *Church Leadership: Vision, Team, Culture, and Integrity,* was described by Rosabeth Moss Kanter of Harvard Business School in her preface to the book as "an invaluable guide to leadership in the church." Leadership author Burt Nanus, emeritus professor at the University of Southern California, said the book is "the best work I have seen on the leadership of religious institutions." Among his more recent books are *The Right Questions for Church Leaders* and *Sustaining While Disrupting: The Challenge of Congregational Innovation*.

Lovett is a graduate of Millsaps College, Perkins School of Theology, Southern Methodist University, and Wesley Theological Seminary. He holds honorary degrees from three colleges and universities. Lovett can be reached at lovettw@wesleyseminary.edu.

OTHER BOOKS FROM
BARRY Z. POSNER

The Leadership Challenge • ISBN: 978-1-119-73612-7

Encouraging the Heart • ISBN: 978-1-394-30390-8

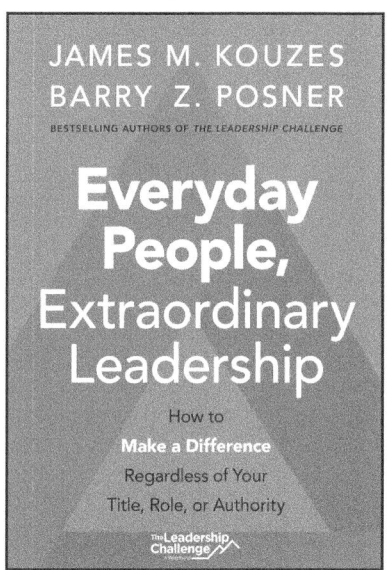

Everyday People, Extraordinary Leadership
• ISBN: 978-1-119-68701-6

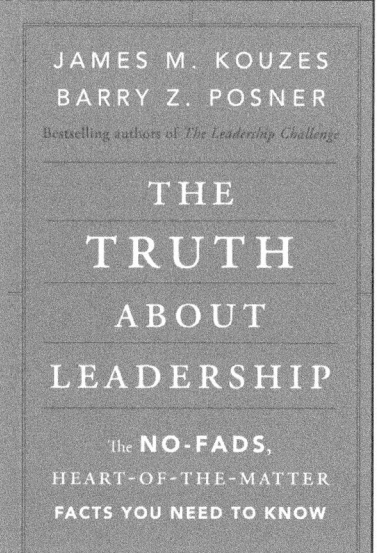

The Truth About Leadership • ISBN: 978-0-470-63354-0